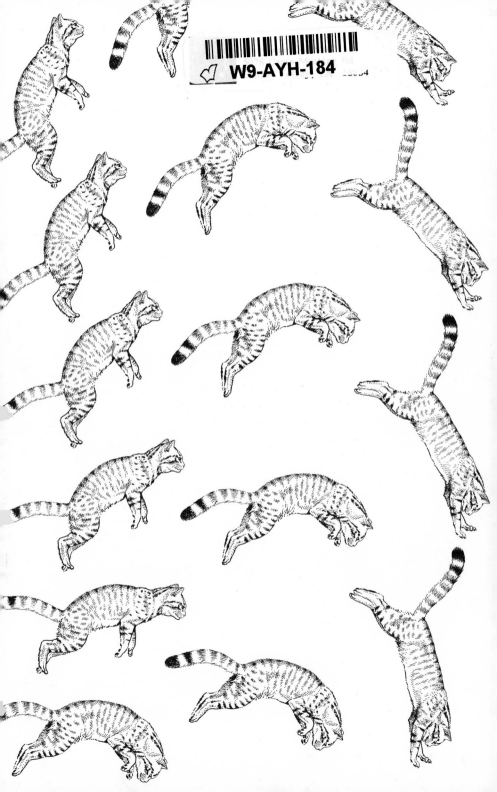

WILDCATS

WILDCATS

•MIKE TOMKIES•

with illustrations by
DENYS OVENDEN

Whittet Books

First published 1991
Text © 1991 by Mike Tomkies
Illustrations © 1991 by Denys Ovenden
Whittet Books Ltd, 18 Anley Road, London W14 0BY

Design by Richard Kelly

Denys Ovenden would like to express his gratitude to the late Dr Nigel
Easterbee for his assistance with reference material for the illustrations.

British Library Cataloguing in Publication Data

Tomkies, Mike, *1928 –*
    Wildcats.
    1. Scotland. Highlands. Wildcats
    I. Title
    599.74428

    ISBN 0–905483–86–3

Typeset by Litho Link Ltd, Welshpool, Powys, Wales
Printed in Great Britain by Biddles of Guildford

Contents

Acknowledgments	7
Introduction	9
What is a wildcat?	11
What's the difference between a wildcat and a domestic one?	17
The wildcat in Britain	23
Senses	31
How ferocious are they?	33
The wildcat menu	37
Are they a danger to livestock?	41
How they hunt	43
Territory and dens	51
Caterwaul	59
Courtship and mating	61
Breeding	63
Development of young	68
Raising young	69
Enemies	72
Can a wildcat be tamed?	74
Can I see a wildcat?	76
Do wildcats interbreed with feral domestics?	78
How is the wildcat doing now?	94
Mystery black cats	97
Selected bibliography	102
Index	104

Acknowledgments

The author would like to acknowledge the help of various individuals and bodies in connection with the preparation of this book: the Mammal section, British Museum of Natural History, for permission to examine their wildcat pelts, Mrs S. Bevis of the London Zoological Society library, John B. Murray for the Royal Scottish Museum pelt measurements, Daphne M. Hills for her papers on the black cats, the late Geoffrey Kinns for general comments, and, last but by no means least, the late Dr Nigel Easterbee, of the Nature Conservancy Council, for his papers, distribution map and helpful suggestions.

Introduction

During my twenty-three years of living in wild, remote places, one of the wild creatures that has most fascinated me has been the Scottish wildcat. It is rare, ferocious, and reputedly untameable. When, in 1974, I returned to my Highland home after tracking wild cougar and grizzly bear in Canada and heard my friend Allan MacColl had found two abandoned wildcat kittens in a ditch and wanted me to look after them, I was somewhat dubious — to say the least. However, as I hastily read about them, I realized how little was known. Scientific observation was scant.

I took the two little spitfires home by boat in late July, and soon understood they were too fierce and intractable to be raised as pets. They had to be approached with caution, could usually only be handled when wearing thick gloves. Both being females, I named them Cleo and Patra, and they made their quarters in the woodshed behind the cottage; I allowed them freedom to come and go. From there I was able to observe their dawn and dusk forays to learn to hunt and establish territories. If ever they stayed away too long, my gentle Alsatian Moobli could locate them by scent.

By the autumn I felt they might not be hunting well enough to earn their own livings, and offered them to London Zoo for breeding purposes. To my surprise, the zoo did not want them as more space was needed for making bigger, more natural enclosures for the larger mammals like lions, tigers and gorillas. In fact, the zoo had a large wildcat tom for which they were trying to find better accommodation.

The upshot was that instead of losing two wildcats, I acquired another — a spitting, growling malevolence, who never once in his ten years of captivity had shown the slightest liking, or even tolerance, towards those who fed him. Sylvesturr, for so I named him, had only one form of greeting — attack! Even if one was approaching with food, he would leap from his bed, slam down a front paw, and emit a loud spitting *PAAAH!* which sounded like a small charge of exploding dynamite.

As I laboured to make the wildcats strong wild enclosures, my hope that Sylvesturr would one day mate with one of the females seemed a faint one indeed. I gave the tom the largest enclosure, complete with natural rocky den. To the end of this I built a smaller run for the two females, and as Sylvesturr was much larger than they were, I made a hole between the pens just large enough for them to get through to him but too small for him to get into their quarters. (I had read that male wildcats will sometimes kill kittens.) All the time the females ran free, returning to their pen to be fed and to sleep in their den box.

From this accidental and shaky start, my wildcat breeding experiment began, and the detailed personal adventures were told in my book *Wildcat Haven*. Ultimately three litters were raised and nine pure wildcats were released into the wild, after Sylvesturr returned from his first winter in the wilds to mate again with Cleo.

It is on these studies, more recent scientific research, and a great deal more observations in the wild than I have hitherto recorded, that the information in the book is based.

Mike Tomkies
June 1990

What is a wildcat?

This is not so foolish a question as it sounds, for more controversy surrounds the wildcat than any other member of our fauna. Once called 'the British tiger', its reputation for ferocity is legend. However, having bred and released two wildcat families to the wild, I found it is ferocious only when cornered and in self defence or, of course, when making a hunting kill. Otherwise, it will always avoid man, and his dogs, if it can. It may look like a large tabby at first sight but it is genetically different from the domestic cat. The Scottish wildcat, *Felis silvestris*, is descended from

the extinct ancestral species *Felis lunensis*, which was rather like a primitive panther or puma.

The precise origin of the domestic cat is not known for certain but consensus says that it originated from the African wildcat, *Felis lybica* and the south-west Asian *Felis ornata*. It is possible that mixtures also came in from other small wild cats such as *Felis margarita* and *cafra*. Such cats found small prey common near man's dwellings and it is believed they were first domesticated by the Egyptians, prior to 1600 BC, who esteemed their tamed cats as being sacred to the goddess Pasht — from which the name 'Puss' is said to derive. In Dutch and also Gaelic the word 'Pus' also means cat.

The tame cats spread in popularity throughout the Mediterranean area and are believed to have been brought to western Europe and Britain by the Phoenician traders to keep rats and mice down in their ships' stores. Later, the Romans brought them over too for the same purposes, and the first mention of *cattus* in literature was made in AD 350 by Palladius who

Egyptian cat figure.

Felis lybica.

Felis ornata.

described them as being 'useful in granaries'. The Romans took them all over their great Empire. From the large number of domestic cat breeds that exist today, it is clear that they evolved from a large genetic pool. Our household and farm cats have long been valued and way back in the tenth century the Prince of Wales promulgated laws that set the value of cats – a kitten before its eyes were open was worth one penny. From the time they

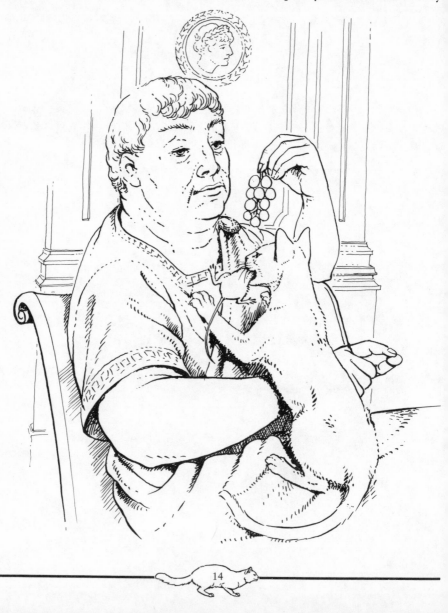

were open to when it caught its first mouse, it was worth two pence, and after its first mouse its value was four pence. For killing a cat, a person could be fined, made to forfeit a milk ewe, or 'pay' into the courts enough grain to cover the cat's body when hung up by the tip of its tail!

No such love was bestowed upon the wildcat, however, and, although it's hard to believe, it was not given full protection by law until as recently

as 1987. Yet in the Scottish wildcat Britain has an indigenous mammal as truly wild, independent and magnificent as any animal in the world. While lynxes, leopards, lions and even tigers can become amenable to man's discipline in captivity, the wildcat does not.

The main controversies surrounding the wildcat are: Can the wildcat, like the domestic, have more than one brood a year, and does it do so in the wild? Can it be tamed at all? Does the wildcat interbreed with feral domestics? Is it related to the 'new' species, the big golden-eyed wild black cats that have been found in recent years? These are just a few of the questions answered in this book.

What's the difference between a wildcat and a domestic one?

The wildcat is generally bigger and stronger than a domestic tabby, its most distinctive feature being a thick, bushy, black-ringed tail which ends in a very blunt black tip.

The fur is a fawny grey and is longer and softer than in the domestic cat. The guard hairs, some over two inches long, are generally whitish grey or dark browny-black, with the flank stripes formed by concentrations of dark hairs. Beneath the guard hairs lies a thick-growing fine wool-like fur, varying from yellow-grey to orangey buff, the latter especially marked on the insides of the thighs and the lower inside of the front legs. The belly fur, sometimes frosty white between the front legs, is short and greyish but lined below the flanks with ochraceous buff and there are dark grey stripes or patches on the under belly which varies with individuals.

The toe pads, pink at birth, are almost completely black in the adult, and are surrounded by thick short black hairs. These black hair patches extend an inch or two up the rear of the front feet, and sometimes right up to the 'heel' bone on the rear feet. The claws are light horn coloured and, like the feet, are larger in proportion than the domestic cat's. The short hair covering the top of the feet is a light buff and in the sun has a gleaming velvet look. Two broad browny-black bands often partly encircle the forelegs in front of the 'elbows'. The wildcat's limbs are longer in proportion to its body than the dometic's, just as the skull is stronger, broader and more robust.

Edward Hamilton measured wildcat skulls in the late 1890s and found they varied between 3 and 3½ inches (78.5 and 89 mm) in basal length, compared with domestic cats' between 2¾ and 3⅓ inches (73 and 85 mm). In mature wildcats, particularly in males, there is a high nasal arch, giving the animal a slightly convex 'Roman' profile. The teeth are also longer and stronger, particularly the canines; the upper two can be almost three-quarters of an inch long and in mature toms protrude even when the mouth is closed.

The wildcat nose is a bright orangey salmon pink in a prime animal,

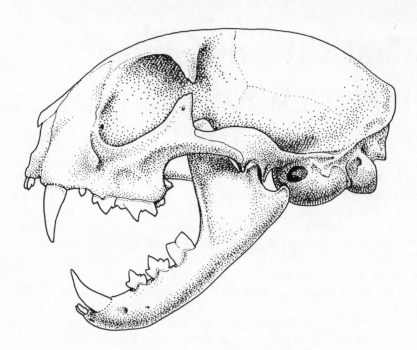

Relative skulls of wildcat (above) *and domestic* (below) *from the side.*

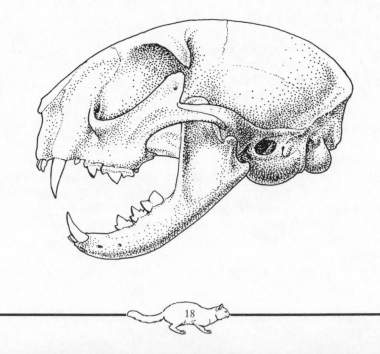

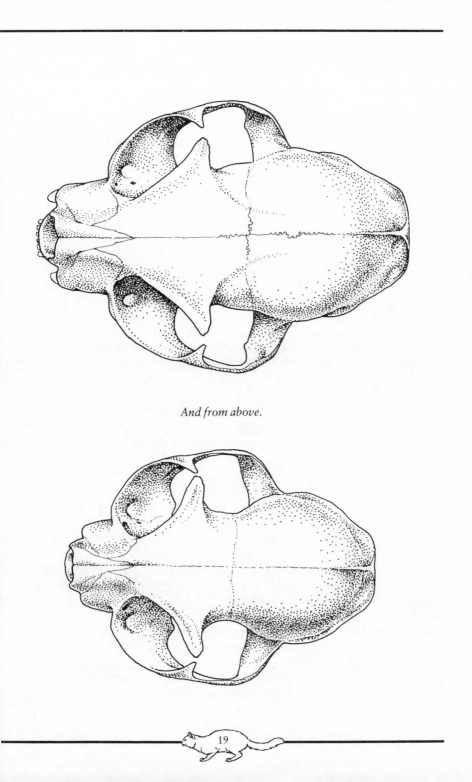

And from above.

though the colour fades in old age. The nose and inner nostrils are edged with a fine black line which extends down to the mouth. The fur of the front upper lips and chin is pale and sometimes there is a small white throat patch. The chin is thicker and more 'determined' looking than in the domestic cat. I believe the animals can signal to each other with their white lips and chins because I often saw my animals opening and closing their mouths when in sight of each other at dusk without emitting a sound. The whiskers are stiff, white, grow in greater profusion than the domestic cats, and often extend far beyond the head width. They are used as 'feelers' when the animal is in narrow places in pitch dark. The lip membranes are black but the inside of the mouth and the rasped tongue are a far brighter red than in the domestic cat. The large eyes have yellow-gold irises which seem to grow paler with age, and no British animal's eyes are more expressive of mood — from rage and ferocity to peaceful relaxation and pleasure when basking in the sun. I noticed the pupils stay rounder longer than those of domestic cats in similar light conditions. They also expand to full roundness in bright daylight when they sense danger, are afraid or in the last stages of a hunt. This tendency to greater roundness may perhaps link wildcats more closely than domestics with the big 'cats' like lions, tigers and pumas, whose pupils do not contract to vertical slits.

On the wildcat's forehead is usually a distinct but unjoined 'M' (the inner ends not meeting in the centre) and a pair of dark lines extend from the eyes to below the ears. The widely spaced ears, held down rather than back when angry, are light tawny, front-edged with dark brown, rimmed with yellow buff, and sometimes end with longer dark hairs at the tip, though this could hardly be called a tuft. From the crown of the head and down the nape are four, rarely five, dark lines which peter out before the shoulders. Between the shoulder blades are usually two, rarely three, strong dark parallel dashes and from them, about an inch away, a dark line runs along the spine to the tail. Occasionally this line breaks into three though the lower lines are often not joined and consist of paler dashes and indistinct spots. The wildcat undergoes an early spring moult to a lighter summer coat (pelage), which helps disguise it better amid the herbage in the increased light. There is another slighter moult in late summer, before the darker pelage of winter, which grows from the end of October, through November and early December.

The tail is often described as short but my research proved that in the finest specimens it usually exceeds half the head and body length; it is, however, shorter than the domestic cat's. Its broad black or blackish rings

Wildcat and pawprint.

vary in number, usually between three and five, though in multi-ringed animals the rings nearest the root are usually indistinct. The wildcat's tail, with its distinctly separate rings, contrasts greatly with the thin, tapering, unevenly striped or blotched tail of the domestic tabby.

In 1943, J.C. Kirk and R. Wagstaffe published the measurements of 107 wildcats, of which only five were females. The average head and body length of the males was 23¼ inches (589 mm) (smallest 14⅜ inches/365 mm, largest 25½ inches/653 mm; the average tail length being 12¼ inches/315 mm) (shortest 8¼ inches/210 mm, longest 13⅓ inches/342 mm). The figures for the five females — average head and body length 22⅓ inches/571 mm; average tail length 12¼ inches/311 mm — reveal a similar picture, and also confirm they are generally considerably smaller animals than the toms.

The biggest wildcats

The heaviest recorded wildcat in the British Museum of Natural History in London is a 1934 tom from Ardgay, Ross-shire, which measured 24⅝ inches (63 cm) head and body, plus a 14 inch (36 cm) long tail, and weighed 15 lb 10 oz (7 kilos). However, there are four longer cats whose weights were not recorded, including a 1925 male from Spean Bridge, Inverness-shire, with a 30⅓ inch (77 cm) head and body, and a 13⅓ inch (33 cm) tail.

My own tom wildcat weighed 16 lb (7.25 kilos) and measured 42½ ins (108 cm) from nose to tail tip; but being captive (up to the time I measured him) he had more fat on him than he would have had in the wild. Kirk and Wagstaffe published in 1943 the weights of 102 male wildcats between 1919 and 1939 and found they varied greatly, from 6½ to 15¼ lb (3 to 7 kilos). But much larger wildcats than any of the above have been recorded, including one noted by Millais which was 46 inches (117 cm) long in October 1899 at Kinlochmoidart, Inverness-shire. One monster weighing over 32 lb (14½ kilos) has been recorded from the East Carpathian mountains in Rumania. The historian Berwick recorded a wildcat 'upwards of five feet' from Cumberland long before they were extinct in England. Wright's edition of Buffon describes the Wild or Wood Cat as measuring 'two feet round the body and, including the tail which is about half a yard long, is about four feet in length.'

The wildcat in Britain

Wildcats co-existed with cave lions, mammoths, bears, wolves and reindeer for thousands of years before the domestic cat was introduced to western Europe around 1200 BC. They formerly lived all over England, Wales and Scotland, though they never inhabited Ireland, and their fossilized remains have been found in Pleistocene era deposits up to two million years old. Bones have been unearthed at places like the Weald at Ightham in Kent, Grays Thurrock in Essex, the Bleadon caves of the

Their thick-furred skins were used for lining clothes.

Mendips, the Creswell Crags in Derbyshire, and Ravenscliff in Glamorgan.

Widespread in England and Wales up to the end of the 15th century, wildcats had various nicknames, like 'cat of the mountains' (it is still called the *Gato Montes* in Spain), 'the wood cat', 'the British tiger' or 'the Bore Cat'. Around 1127 their thick-furred skins were being used for lining clothes. Kings John, Richard II and Edward II and III all granted licences for hunting wolves, foxes, martens and wildcats in many English countries. Edward Hamilton recorded that some parts of the wildcat were used as medical aids, the flesh being 'helpful to the gout'. Its fat was 'hot, dry, emollient, discursive and anodyne', and 'mixed with palm oil and oil of aniseed, it dissolves tumours, eases pain, prevails against nodes on the skin and the cold gout'. As if that was not enough, 'certain excrements made into a powder and mixed with mustard seed, juice of onions and bear's grease enough to form an ointment, cures baldness and the alopaecia.' I am not sure how rubbing powdered wildcat shit on one's head as a cure for baldness would go down today!

Powdered wildcat dung was a baldness cure.

The wildcat's independence and ferocity were well known even in those distant days and in 1606 Shakespeare, playing on the word 'cat' in *The Taming Of The Shrew*, had Petruchio say to Katherina, 'Thou must be married to no man but me for I am he and born to tame you Kate. And bring you from a wildcat to a Kate, conformable as other household Kates.'

Slowly, increasing human population and the felling and burning of forest cover from the Iron Age to the 19th century for timber and grazing land drove the wildcat north to its final fastnesses in Scotland. In England, wildcats were extinct in Northampton by 1712, considerably diminished in Cumberland by 1790 (the last one killed near Loweswater in the Lake District in 1843), and extinct in the Hambleton Hills, Yorkshire, by 1881. In Wales, they were almost extinct by 1826 but one was trapped in Montgomeryshire in 1864.

After their extinction in England and Wales, and after the notorious Highland Clearances, the industrial rich of the 19th century travelled north to Scotland on the new railways to their freshly acquired estates to pursue the sports of hunting grouse, deer, rabbits and hares. The estates employed thousands of gamekeepers who regarded all predators as vermin; the final and direct persecution of the wildcat had begun. They were snared, trapped and shot in huge numbers. Keepers, regarding vermin as their own 'perks', could get a sovereign a time for a wildcat in taxidermist shops. Later the cats were also persecuted for alleged predation on lambs and occasional raids on unhoused poultry — for which some folk would still shoot them today.

In 1881, naturalist Harvie Brown recorded the wildcat as then extinct south-east of a rough line from Oban, up the Brander Pass to Dalmally, along the Perth border, including Rannoch Moor, to the junction of the counties of Perth, Forfar (Angus) and Aberdeen, then north-east to Tomintoul in Banff, then north-west again to Inverness. By the turn of the century many naturalists were predicting its extinction all over Britain. By summarizing the notes of Edward Hamilton, James Ritchie, S.F. Harmer, Edward Step and Harvie Brown, the picture in the early 1900s emerges as follows:

Aberdeen	surviving Glen Tanar until 1875 but almost extinct in county by 1891
Angus (Forfar)	almost extinct by 1850
Argyll	last one killed at Loch Awe in 1864; one

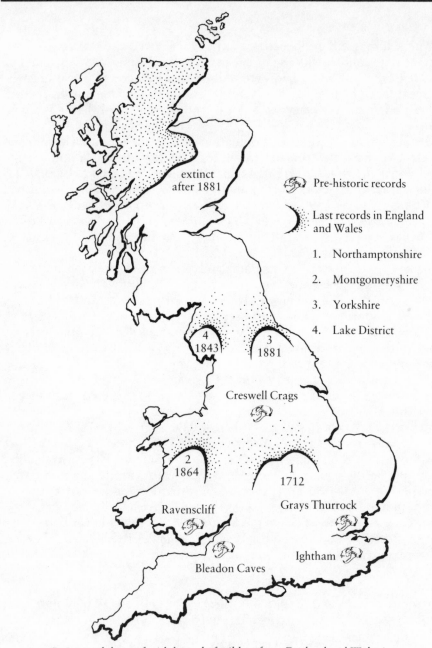

Points and dates of withdrawal of wildcat from England and Wales into nineteenth-century Scotland.

	appeared Glen Orchy 1899, but still rarely found around Ardnamurchan, Sunart, Ardgour and Morvern. Virtually extinct in south Argyll by 1864
Banff	almost extinct by 1850
Berwick	last border wildcat killed near old Cambus 1849
Dumfries	extinct by 1832
Dumbarton	extinct by 1857
Elgin	practically extinct by 1850
Inverness-shire	last wildcats killed at Glenmore in 1873, by 1882 very rare but not extinct in south and central areas, though north and west was its main stronghold in Scotland
Kincardine	a pair killed at Glen Dye in 1850 by which time practically extinct
Kirkcudbright	extinct by 1832
Moray	one killed 1860 near Forres, but a few still existing
Nairn	almost extinct by 1850 (one killed at Cawdor, undated, measured 3 ft 9 inches)
Perthshire	last killed at Atholl 1857, Ben More 1864 and believed extinct in south by 1870. A wildcat killed twelve miles from Perth in 1925 was believed to have been part of a new spread south from Lochs Ericht and Laggan, Inverness-shire, where it had re-appeared 1912
Ross and Cromarty	last one killed in east Ross 1873, believed extremely rare in west. One killed Dornoch Firth 1912
Stirling	extinct in most parishes by 1842
Sutherland	dwindling by 1880
Wigtownshire	extinct by 1832

Through the early 1900s the wildcat clung on in its last remote areas in north-west Argyll, Kintyre, Stirling, west Inverness-shire and western Ross. A few of the more intelligent landowners like the Earls of Seafield realizing so rare and fascinating a mammal was worth the loss of a few brace of sport grouse, afforded it some protection. But the Great War was its main saviour, just as it helped other persecuted creatures like pine martens and golden eagles, for many keepers were away after human targets.

The plantings by the new Forestry Commission after World War I gave the wildcat population, still endangered, a further boost, for not only were they tolerated for their predation on rabbits, voles and ground birds which ate seedlings, but the woods gave them new shelter and encouraged an increase in a large variety of prey. World War II also provided some amnesty, and in recent years the growth of private forestry has further helped. The wildcat was also tolerated on deer hunting estates for its feeding on voles and rabbits which ate the grass, and hares whose sudden scatterings from hunters spoiled deer stalks.

Not until a 1961 survey was another attempt made to assess wildcat populations. This was conducted by Dr David Jenkins from Aberdeen University, who received 135 full replies to 248 detailed questionnaires he sent to estates in Scotland. A brief summary of his findings:

Aberdeen	wildcats uncommon but present in upper Deeside, in smaller numbers in upper Strathdon and reappearing in Glen Muick. No increase
Angus	common locally, particularly in Glen Clova, but spreading into Glen Lethnot, Glen Esk and possibly Glen Prosen after 1955
Argyll	still rare but perhaps increasing in the newly forested areas
Ayrshire	none known
Banff	a few on low ground but could be widespread over higher ground
Caithness	uncommon, but six killed by one estate in 1960
Inverness-shire	widely distributed and quite plentiful in woods and moors. Probably increased during World War II but reduced again when keepers returned from service. (One estate, Glenmazeran, killed

	86 wildcats in the years 1950, 1953, 1955, 1958 and 1960: 35 of them in 1958)
Kincardine, Kinross	rare or absent
Moray and Nairn	few wildcats over low ground but there was a sudden remarkable increase on some moors around 1957 to 1959
Perthshire	widely distributed over moors but in low numbers. No widespread increase
Ross and Cromarty	uncommon, no recent change
Stirling	Dr J.D. Lockie reported four wildcat sightings, and one being trapped at Fintry, a notable extension to their south-eastern range
Sutherland	uncommon, no evidence of recent change

This was the information on the slightly improved wildcat status that could be best obtained up to 1961. After that the Mammal Society and Biological Records Centre both collected information on distribution of wildcats up to 1977. From this it was clear the wildcat still had a long way to go to reach its previous southern range before 1900 — where it was found eastwards from the tip of Kintyre, Ayrshire, Renfrew, more rarely in Lanark, Dumfries and Berwick. The map shows that there were populations between 1900 and 1959 in north Kintyre, central and north Argyll, south-west and north-east Perth, with scattered remnants widely distributed over Inverness-shire, and a few individual sightings in south-east Aberdeen, western Ross and south-east Sunderland. But where wildcats depended on rabbits in the north-west generally, a surge of myxomatosis in the mid 1950s set back their recovery considerably. Even so, sightings up to 1977 showed a spread to areas where they had been rare for well over a century. At that time the greatest numbers were in north and central Argyll, south-west Perth, north Stirling, south Aberdeen, north Angus, south and north-east Inverness-shire, with a great increase in Moray and Banff. Ross and Cromarty now had fair populations, widely distributed, which had spread into south and central Sutherland.

In 1983 the Nature Conservancy Council took on the difficult task of surveying the wildcat, and concluded that while the animal had re-colonized more of its former central-areas, the spread had largely ceased. Also a complication arose: the discovery of the extent of hybridization.

Wildcats worldwide

The wildcat is a creature of the northern hemisphere but is not found in America or Canada — where the bobcat and the Canadian lynx occupy its kind of terrain and niche in the animal kingdom. The European wildcat is found in France, Spain, Germany, most of south and central Europe and Pyrenees (but not Scandinavia or Finland) including Czechoslovakia and Rumania, and then across west and south Russia. The Scottish wildcat is usually larger and darker-coloured than the types in south and central Europe.

Senses

The wildcat hunts its prey principally by sight but it also uses its acute hearing. Several times I saw my wildcats locate slow-worms, lizards and even shrews tunnelling through grass roots, by the sounds they made. Sight was the final confirmation before the death pounce. Their hearing is paramount for warning of danger. Sometimes when I was watching my cats sitting outside the cottage in the sun, I would see their heads turn round suddenly to look up the loch, then they would flee back to their open pen. When I went outside I could hear or see nothing but almost a minute later I would hear the sound of a boat engine heading our way. Their hearing was far more sensitive than mine.

Some naturalists believe wildcats disdain carrion, unlike foxes and badgers. But while they will not feed from 'high' carcasses like those of winter-dead red deer as will fox, crow or raven, my wildcats proved they could scent such venison (or meat I put out for them) from at least 50

Shrews may be located by sound.

yards. Sometimes, if the wind was steady and strong enough, they could locate such food up to 250 yards away. Their olfactory abilities are most important; naturalist Lea MacNally once saw a wildcat stalking a rabbit, on the far side of thick herbage, entirely by scent.

Sometimes I have watched wildcats at night on the Ardnamurchan peninsula by the aid of a powerful torch on a long lead that works from a car battery. Oddly, the animals seem little put out by a sudden bright light, and will even work a zigzag route towards you if you blow on one of those rabbit squeakers designed to attract foxes. While doing this one night I just caught sight of a large tom heading for a rabbit burrow, down which he doubtless hoped to find a fresh dinner. Just as he reached the entrance he stopped, and several times poked his head into the hole and withdrew it, before finally disappearing. It was clear he was using those exceptionally long white whiskers as feelers in so dark and narrow a place. A wildcat can get through anywhere its head can, and, as I found out occasionally to my cost, is an accomplished escapologist.

How ferocious are they?

The renowned ferocity of the wildcat is purely defensive. Far from being 'utterly fearless' or likely to 'spring at your throat like a tiger' as one naturalist wrote in a national paper in early 1977, the wildcat is afraid of man and dogs and will do its utmost to avoid or escape either. When it *is* at bay, it does not arch its back, fluff out all its fur with upraised tail, presenting as large as possible *side* view to bluff its opponent as to its size, as a domestic cat does. It fluffs its fur certainly, but usually backs into a corner, against a rock, tree or bush, keeps its tail down and rears as high as it can to present a ferocious *frontal* aspect. With ears down, fangs bared, deep low growls punctured by violent spits at every movement of the enemy, it is here that its extraordinarily long *ulnae* (top foreleg bones)

Wildcat at bay.

come into play. It seems to raise its front and head to twice normal heigh
its big claws ready to rake and slash at any attacker.

Only if it is cornered or surprised at close quarters where it feels
cannot escape, or caught in a trap, will it set up this devastating front
display. Even then its main aim is to shock the enemy back onto its heel
so it can make a lightning spring past and escape, still avoiding contac
Only if bodily contact is made, or dog or man tries to prevent its escape c
kill it, will it actually fight. Then, indeed, it will fight like a tiger.

Charles St John, who described how he stumbled upon one and kille
it with a staff and the aid of three Skye terriers, wrote, 'I never saw a
animal fight so desperately, or one which was so difficult to kill. If a tam
cat has nine lives, a wildcat must have a dozen.' St John was one of th
best of the early hunter/naturalists and wrote superbly about th
Highlands, but why he felt he had to bash to death with his staff a wildca
which already had three dogs, each heavier than itself, also intent on it
death, he did not explain. They did many foolish things to wildlife in th
1830s and 40s — he even admitted shooting golden eagles.

The wildcat is a redoubtable opponent and its thicker skull, bigger jaw
and longer teeth enable it to give a harder bite than any domestic cat. Bu
it is no worse than that from a cornered otter, and nothing like the terribl
bite that the much-loved badger can inflict, powerful enough to crack
terrier's skull.

The wildcat mother is aggressive and fearless in defence of her young
When my first female had her second litter of kits, I saw her once fac
down a fox that had come prowling nearby. She advanced straight out c
her den, fur and tail bristling, and with loud growls advanced slowl
towards it then stopped, glaring straight at it. And the fox wilted befor
her savage stare, and retreated.

Pioneer naturalist Seton Gordon recorded how an eagle was seen t
stoop several times down upon a wildcat on a rock with legs and talon
outstretched but twice the wildcat leaped into the air, striking out with it
claws. This deterred the eagle for although it stooped some thirty times i
did not go close afterwards. A watching keeper traced the wildcat to he
den, and felt it odd the cat should expose itself to the eagle's attacks whe
as far as he could see the kittens were not out in the open. Perhaps it wa
trying to deter the eagle from coming that way again!

The late photographer Geoffrey Kinns was given an eye-witnes
account of a wildcat springing onto the back of an eagle after it ha
snatched one of its kittens, both being shot in the air by a watching keeper

It appears male wildcats tend to avoid each other for I have neve

It can fight off a golden eagle.

Speedy at escape.

known of a wildcat fight in the wild, which would be a noisy affair. When wildcats are kept in groups in zoos or safari parks and there is more than one male, fights are seldom seen.

Perhaps one reason why an animal so capable of *war* does not actually fight very often, is because it is so fast on its feet. Once, when we were tracking after my young wildcats in high bracken so I could check their welfare, my Alsatian cornered a seven-week-old male kit, which promptly went into the defensive display. Carefully, I knelt on the hem of my jacket, then threw it over the hissing bundle and pinned it down. But when I peeled back the jacket there was nothing there! We had heard nothing, felt nothing, seen not one stem of bracken quiver, yet that young wildcat had shot away so fast neither mine nor the dog's eyes had been able to follow.

The wildcat menu

The wildcat's food consists of rabbits (for which it will wait patiently near burrows) and mountain hares; in the rare instances when wildcats are found in places without rabbits, small mammals such as field voles and mice form an important part of the diet. Field voles can do great damage in young forestry plantations as their populations can cyclically grow to 'plague' proportions when they eat all the young seedlings and strip tender bark from baby trees. Voles can also be hosts for the early stages of a tick that transmits the 'louping ill' disease to hill sheep. Most medium-sized predators do not like shrews because of the distasteful scent glands along their flanks, but wildcats will certainly eat them when hungry — without hesitation. They will, however, often rake out and leave the dark green gall bladders of small rodents.

Also taken are birds up to the size of woodpigeon or occasional game birds (8 per cent of the diet in the East Carpathian mountains, Romania) and infrequently eggs and nestlings of ground-nesters. Most prey is taken on the ground but my females three times brought chaffinch eggs back to their quarters, which must have entailed a climb.

Catching a fish.

Wildcats will hunt the edges of lochs and burns where ground birds take their young to drink in summer; ducks, mergansers, and other water and marsh birds all fall victim to them. I once found the remains of a barn owl, far from its natural habitat and probably weakened by its winter search for a home in sparse woodland, that had been killed and eaten by a wildcat. I knew this, not only by the tell-tale tracks and scratch marks on a nearby birch, but also because the feathers had been raked out — a wildcat hallmark. A fox usually clips them off.

Squirrels, frogs, slow worms, lizards, rats, moles, water voles and even occasional weasels are taken. Certainly they like eating eels. Sometimes an eel would get caught up in the wrong end of my 100-yard-long water pipe, and there was no way I could get it out alive. I would nail the carcass to a stump outside the wildcats' quarters and within minutes one would catch its scent and come out to get it. Eels fill their gills with water and travel like snakes overland in dewy grass when they want to go from lochs to ponds or burns to higher lochans, or to negotiate sheer waterfalls in the burns, and they become easy prey for wildcats at such times. Fish travelling over shallow rocky riffles can also be caught by both foxes and wildcats.

Beetles, grasshoppers and other large juicy insects are not despised, nor are larger moths which are sometimes chased and swiped down by the

Wildcat fantasy.

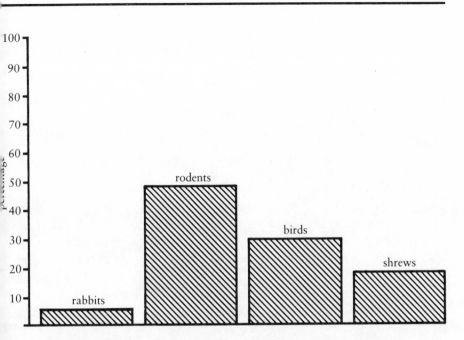

Wildcat diet in West Scotland (data from Hewson 1983); main items only.

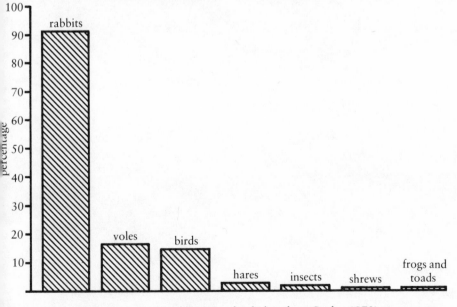

Wildcat diet in North East Scotland (data from Corbet 1978).

paws, especially by youngsters. One of my females knocked down a rare giant wood wasp once, which ended up in the collection of the British Museum of Natural History, London! Carrion, of red deer or old sheep that have died in the hills may be a fairly important food item in winter, especially as the suspicious fox tends to leave a new carcass alone for several days. The wildcat is quite capable of standing its front feet on a carcass and rending the skin upwards although it has relatively small front teeth, but it seems to prefer to take time to cut and chisel away the skin instead, far more neatly than a fox.

I have found wildcat scats in the wild containing vegetation. The intestinal canals of wildcats can be up to a third shorter in proportion to those of domestics. They probably get sufficient roughage from prey (fur, feathers and bones) without the need for vegetable matter. But they have been known to eat grass, dry hay or even old dry bracken stalks.

Are they a danger to livestock?

Reliable reports of isolated individuals taking very young lambs have been made — but they are rare. When these particular individuals are removed, the lamb killing has ceased. However, one wildcat I was trying to tame was actually afraid of an injured lamb that I was looking after. When the lamb, hefty and about two months old, sought the shade in the gap between the woodshed and the cottage wall on hot June days, the wildcat refused to enter the shed which was her main quarters.

Occasionally an old or hungry wildcat, especially in the cold months, will leave its home territory and haunt outlying farmhouses and crofts if it finds loose poultry the owner does not shut up at night in a predator-proof hut. Usually it removes just one to eat but can return for more of the easy prey until the irate owner traps or shoots it, or, better, looks after his birds.

Waiting by rabbit hole.

One crofter shepherd not far from where I lived decided there were too many rabbits on his land and they were eating the grass intended for his sheep. Instead of shooting some for the 'pot', he journeyed to an area where a new outbreak of myxomatosis had occurred, obtained an infected rabbit and shoved it into his biggest warren. The disease caught, spread, and by winter most of the rabbits were dead. He was outraged when a wildcat came to raid his hen-run and poultry house each night, yet it was his own fault for thus depriving the cat of its natural and favourite prey! He called in a keeper, who trapped the wildcat (later letting it go). That spring the crofter also lost some lambs to foxes, for they too were short of rabbit prey.

Predation by wildcats on red deer calves is rare; the calf can run fast at only two days old. Occasionally one of the usual twins born to roe deer may be taken after a chance meeting in the woods, but it would be most uncommon. Indeed, I have never seen the remains of red deer calves, lambs or roe deer kids outside wildcat dens.

In the winter of 1976, a wildcat killed a large goose at Kinlochmoidart, and, unable to carry it away, ate part of it on a nearby path. But such losses are as nothing compared with those inflicted by feral domestic cats or the occasional sheepdog on the loose (which is commoner than suspected).

How they hunt

One misty dawn on a Scottish moor near the sea I was lucky enough to see a wildcat tom hunting rabbits. Using almost every sense he possessed, prowling slowly and warily through the rushes and tussocks, his tawny, grey-striped body looked almost as large as a roe deer's and appeared to mingle with the background. He worked his way upwind towards a small green pasture where the rabbits were grazing.

Every so often he paused with a paw upraised, scenting the air and the nearest rabbit, and listening hard with pricked ears. As he approached he

Hunting rabbits.

flattened his ears and peered through the grasses, appearing to locate his victim by sight. Then, keeping even lower, his bushy, striped tail just brushing the ground, he crept slowly closer, keeping out of sight behind the last tuft. Gathering his long hind legs beneath his belly, he launched a lightning attack.

The rabbit saw the wildcat coming but seemed paralysed by his devastating speed and in three bounds the cat was upon it. The cat appeared to deliver a stunning smash to the rabbit's head with his right foot, hooked both sets of claws round its body, then sank his teeth into the neck. He hit the rabbit with such force that both animals rolled over twice,

The lightning pounce.

Airborne after a bird.

and I fancied I heard brief low growls as the cat also delivered raking slashes with his hind legs. Then in a trice the wildcat lifted the now-dead rabbit in its jaws and loped heavily off into the undergrowth. This rare sighting showed me just how efficient this animal's hunting skills are. It uses this technique with all its larger prey, like hares and the bigger birds, stalking behind cover as much as possible, keeping low, until it is several yards away, then it bounds forward making the attack as terrifying as possible. With smaller prey like voles or mice it approaches carefully, its tail not twitching like a domestic cat's, until within a yard or so. Then with a lightning bound it pounces, clutches the prey with its claws and holds it down or hauls it back for the death bite, usually in the skull or neck area. It never plays with its victims when they are alive (as does a domestic cat), probably not because of any compassion but because, in the totally wild situation, it does not want its prey to have a chance of escape.

Several times I observed that if my wildcats missed with their first

Nesting black-throated divers and culprit.

pounce at a bird, they would leap high into the air after it, making lightning strokes with both sets of claws, often knocking the bird down from mid air. Certainly the powerful smash of the clawed paw also helps stun victims and when the cat kicks with its hind claws against a larger victim's body it is probably designed to disembowel. This activity constitutes quite a large part of kitten play although they do not exert full force.

In dense undergrowth, in woodland or hill heather and tall tussock grass, where sight is restricted, the wildcat relies more on scent, and also hearing — a rustle instantly alerts it to prey presence. J.G. Millais wrote that wildcats occasionally make a loud scream when hunting which causes the prey to squat down and so be easier to catch. I have known foxes use a similar technique whereby they give a sharp 'yak' bark, and the pocket of warm air expelled by the suddenly squatting bird or mammal helps the fox locate it by scent. I have not seen this myself with the wildcat, though it may be possible. Sometimes they will wait in ambush for prey, behind grass or heather tufts near small trails or burrows.

On several occasions I saw my wildcats run into thick herbage, then smite down moths, grasshoppers and other large insects they had disturbed. The one I tried to tame would come to my lighted window at night, attracted by the moths that flew to the lamp's glare, then catch them and chomp them up like cornflakes.

Wildcats can catch small fish in the shallows, and also water voles, usually when they are swimming to shore. They will swim readily themselves if there is a good reason — to cross a river, a small sea inlet, or to reach an island where they think or know there is prey. One early summer dawn in a sea loch near my home, I saw some terns screaming and constantly diving upon the rocky islet where they had their young. As my boat drew near, I was astonished to see a wildcat leap into the water and swim rapidly away, its head and shoulders well above the surface, ears flat as if ensuring water would not get into them. It swam fifteen yards to the main island, then bounced off into the woods without even pausing to shake itself. It had certainly been after the nestlings which were walking between their nests and would have been easy to spot.

One June a pair of rare black-throated divers I was watching from a hide on a fresh-water islet did not return to their nest. They were paddling along offshore, showing 'bereaved' behaviour — constantly setting their heads behind their wings. Eventually I went over to the nest — to find the eggs had been chewed up near it, only shell fragments remaining. A pine marten would have carried the eggs away and on the rocky islet's shore no footprints showed. The mainland was only some fifty yards away so I boated over, searched the shore, and soon found evidence of the culprits.

There in the sand were the unmistakeable four-toed prints of big wildcat feet; as the cat had almost reached the tree line, it had broken into a run, for the last two prints were deeper, splayed out and the claw marks showed clearly. Knowing the wildcat's ability to swim, I had little doubt that it had spotted the divers going to and from the nest, for these birds share incubation duties, and had deduced there would be big fat eggs there! One very rare creature preying upon another may seem tragic, but such is the way of the wild.

The wildcat is solitary by nature and hunts alone. There is some published evidence that they will occasionally hunt together but I suggest this springs from brief sightings of male and female together in the breeding period, late February to mid March. I feel it unlikely they would hunt as a *team*, as do lions.

In summer, during one of my freed wildcat tom's visits to my wood, the nest of a collared dove had been robbed of one egg and the bark of the slim oak tree, up which no fox could have climbed, had been deeply scratched. There were a few feathers scattered about which looked as if they had come from a dove's belly plumage. I reconstructed the whole scene in my mind's eye. On visiting the wood, the powerful old tom had perhaps seen the bird fly in at dusk, had waited in a thicket until near dark, hatching his plan of attack. Then, stalking slowly, silently, towards the tree, he had gathered his long powerful back legs together, had sprung like a lightning tawny blur onto the trunk, made a couple of scraping scrabbles on the bark with his thick talons, and had seized the dozing bird before it had known what hit it. Whether he had returned another time to take the egg I do not know but crows would have taken both eggs. As I said earlier, the other wildcats brought chaffinch eggs back to their quarters. All this is not sufficient evidence to prove that wildcats will raid tree nests but they have been known, as Millais records, to make their homes in large deserted bird's nests and, being excellent climbers, it is possible.

The wildcat is usually described as a nocturnal hunter, but I feel crepuscular would be more exact as all my wildcats were most active for an hour or two after sunset and an hour before dawn — coinciding with the main movements of their small mammal prey. However, they will also hunt by day, especially in the autumn when starting to grow their thick winter coats, and to lay up fat to help them through the harsh Highland winter. My first wild sightings were of wildcats hunting in open patches between heather sprigs a good two hours after dawn, though it is rare to see them hunting by day in summer after 8.30 am or before 8 pm; they spend most of the day resting up. They sometimes bask in the sun on mossy boulders or on broad tree branches, rather like leopards. They even seem to like to prop up their heads in forked twigs, which looks most uncomfortable!

They hunt, depending on their individual terrains, in woodland, among rocky cairns and mountain slides, and on open moors, with great adaptability. They also hunt in light rain or on crisp snow but not during heavy storms or winds unless driven out by hunger; they distrust waving foliage and fear noise and falling twigs and branches. Most of their intended prey is under shelter anyway at such times.

Wildcats cover uneaten remains of kills, often hauling them under long heather clumps or small bushes, and arranging debris cover to resemble the surrounding terrain. This not only hides carcasses from other predators such as crow, raven, buzzard or fox, but also reduces the scent, helps to keep the meat fresher and also protects it from spoiling slugs and insect scavengers. Females with kits old enough to accompany them take great pains to cover up uneaten food, to return to it next evening from a temporary den.

Territory and dens

The figure of 150 acres (60 to 70 hectares) is often quoted as being a wildcat's normal territory but this seems too simple a generalization. Much must surely depend on the type of terrain (woodland, treed burn and gorge, open moorland, sea coast are all acceptable to the wildcat), the density or availability of prey, plus the age and ability of an individual cat to hunt efficiently. On open moorland, for instance, the range could be as much as 500-600 acres. My observations suggest that wildcats are not

Basking in a tree.

Droppings on a prominent place.

particularly territorial but until a research team works full time on individual cats and families with light radio-tracking equipment over several years (and this would be *extremely* difficult in the rocky hilly Highlands) information upon territory will be largely guesswork. Males wander widely in spring, as did my freed tom, during the breeding period, but females with young are naturally compelled to stay in smaller areas. Males that are not paired up, or do not know of a particular female, probably wander for miles to try and locate one, and certainly one that will accept them!

Droppings, dark grey, grey-green or brown, are usually covered on snow, sand, gravel or shingle but seldom on grass or beds of broken-down bracken. Sometimes they are found, fox-like, on a prominent place, a mossy rock or old stump, as if left deliberately. P. Bang, P. Dahlstrom and W. Lindeman suggest that marking with faeces and urine define the outskirts of territory; and that *inside* the territory scats are buried. This seems feasible, and it has been estimated that wildcats bury only about 9 per cent of their faeces, far less than are buried by domestic cats — though, being well fed on the whole, and so needing smaller territories, these may just be keeping their little gardens clean and tidy!

Male wildcats spray urine, which is scented by a special rear gland, onto

(Right) *Typical wildcat den.*

vegetation, rocks and trees, to mark territory. Females also squat and release scent from anal glands along with their urine. It is clear all these signs have many uses — to warn off other males, to avoid other males, to inform females of a male's presence (and maybe status and sexuality or state), and by females in heat (oestrus) to inform males of the fact and their presence. I do not believe that wildcats stay in pairs all through the year, for both sexes are solitary by nature. However, their coming together when the female is in oestrus surely cannot be left to chance meeting by sight and body scent alone. Cougars (pumas) in North America and Canada make special 'scratch piles' of debris mixed with

Wildcat territory.

their faeces and urine for these purposes.

Claw 'sharpening' marks are occasionally found on small tree trunks, usually hard birch; although the animals do have scent glands in their feet, I do not feel the primary purpose of this is to mark territory, though it may have that secondary effect. Cats' claws are retractile, which prevents them being blunted from constant rubbing on rocks, earth and the hard wood of trees. When they dig them into hard surfaces the purpose is not to actually 'sharpen' them but serves to clean away excess horny outer sheath from the claws, which grow sharp naturally. Having watched my wildcats perform this action many times, I believe that the exercise — when they

Scent marking.

haul down heavily on the dug-in claws and scratch deeply — is also to strengthen the sinew and muscle that control the claws, not to mention the arms and shoulders, so the entire forelimb weapons stay strong for hunting. Rather like weight training in humans.

Wildcats make their breeding dens in natural chambers and crevices in ancient rockfalls, small caves, hollow standing or fallen trees, under dry root clusters of stumps or windfalls, in old fox earths or the larger rabbit burrows. Usually they choose dense deciduous or mixed woodland, or the steep treed sides of ravines above burns and rivers. They also have temporary short-stay dens around their territory. Rarely they may use large birds' nests in trees but would not rear young in them. In the extreme north and west where tree cover is scant, they den amid the rocky slides and cairns of the open hill, living and hunting beyond the height to which feral cats will range. In the worst of winter, however, even these 'high' cats will come down to forest cover if there is any within reasonable reach.

Wildcat tracks have been recorded at over 2,000 ft (600 metres) in Scotland and I have found them myself at nearly 1,800 ft (550 metres), and in snow at that. In the warmer climate and far higher mountains of Spain, I have found their tracks at over 5,000 ft (1,500 metres). The ability to live an almost alpine life by some wildcats could be a part response to centuries of persecution by humankind, as they have retreated to places away from man.

Dens are hard to find, for wildcats leave few signs of occupation; no

Exercising claws and sinews.

well trodden paths or dung pits like the badger. They are usually not lined, though the female occasionally makes some effort to rake in heather or dry grass before having her kits. Before he was freed, my old male raked in dry deer hair and made deep bowls of hay in his den in the pens. In the wild I did find his main den but it was at the end of a tunnel so I could not see if he had raked hay in there too. My Alsatian scented out one of his temporary day dens, in a rocky arbour near our west wood, and there was certainly a rough bed of white 'winter' grass in it. Late last century a wild-cat litter was found born on an open bed of bracken at Drumnadrochit, doubtless the exception that proves the rule.

Caterwaul

The wildcat's voice is far more varied and complicated than most people would believe. The kits make a loud piercing note '*Meeoo*' when alarmed and handled at only two days old, which changes to an even louder '*Maow*' at four or five days old. From four days they give a high trilling note when seeking their mother's teats and her warm body. At less than a week old they try to hiss and spit at outside disturbance (before even their eyes are open), but neither is audible to the human ear until the eighth or ninth day. Later, they make a special suckling noise by smacking their lips when already at their mother's body but, waking up suddenly, want some milk. This lip-smacking noise can continue until five months old, when it is often made near the mother's head.

At five or six weeks the kits can give the loud '*Maow*' call when alarmed, but also a still more piercing whistling note '*Wheeoo*' when really frightened. This sound is probably given in the wild if straggling kits are picked up by a fox or eagle. When the kits get caught up in a thicket of brambles or in fencing they warn their mother with a loud squawking '*Mauuw*', a harsh call which is louder but similar to that of a duck grabbed by fox, dog or man.

From eight months the distinctive '*Brrrooo*' trill, which sounds like a sawn-off version of the turtle dove's song, develops. This sound is used for greeting each other, expressing affection, and also to call back the kits when they are not far; but from farther away the wildcat's most-used sound, a loud '*Mau*', is employed.

When the kits are running wild with their mother, a high pitched metallic '*Awroori*' is used, a ventriloquistic call which helps them all keep in touch yet not give away their exact position to possible predators on the kits. Wildcats can and do purr, just as do cougars and lynxes. It is a sudden breathy, clattering sound which often ends suddenly. This purr is slower and louder than that of the domestic cat but is rarely used; only when the animal is in an exceptionally good mood, which is not often in human presence!

The ability to growl, at first like high-pitched whirring dynamos, develops at about a month. As the cats grow older this growl deepens in volume until in an old tom it can sound like the start of a minor earthquake. It is used to display anger, and as a warning before the ferocious spits and foot stamps. The female occasionally emits loud tormented screeches during her oestrus, probably to help locate the male. It is a chilling sound, more unearthly than even the call of a vixen. I never heard my old tom make such sounds but males are reputed to call noisily in the spring, again probably to help contact a female.

Courtship and mating

An exact rutting or oestrus period for the male has not yet been established but my tom went off his food in February and showed more interest in the females when they wandered into his pen to steal his food, always without protest from him. The male's noisiness from early March could be caused by the scent discovery of his mate, or any female if he has no partner, being in oestrus, a period which lasts in the first instance up to ten days.

'Courtship' appears to consist of occasional plaintive mewing, affectionate and mutual head banging, with the male following the female around and frequently nuzzling her, rubbing his head against her flanks. I once observed my paired male and female 'kissing', their heads turned sideways as they bit into each other's mouths, appearing to exchange saliva. In zoos male sexual activity has been known to last from late January, and copulation can continue after pregnancy has begun.

If females do not mate during their first oestrus they can have two more, up to mid or even late May. It is possible to know this without examination for they behave skittishly, growling and rolling over tufts of grass, are more playful, their vaginas swell and the buff fur on the undersides of their thighs gains an orange hue.

Mutual head banging.

And nuzzling flanks.

My own experience seemed to indicate that wildcat males are monogamous; they certainly seem to mate with the same partner each year. Nature writer Frances Pitt recorded that her own wildcat male Satan was so devoted to his mate that he 'rent the air with hideous cries of lamentation whenever she left his quarters. He would not accept any substitute. I several times introduced other females but he attacked them at sight . . . He never cast an attentive eye on any female save his mate.' My second female tried hard but failed dismally to arouse the tom's interest after he had mated with her thinner and wilder sister. And the following year he came back from the wild to mate with the same female again.

Breeding

Here we enter controversy. The question is, can wildcats, like domestics, have two or even three litters a year, and if so, do they in the wild? For years many naturalists believed they could, and did. My own experiences lead me to take sides with the few who thought the true Scottish wildcat, as has been proven for its German counterpart, normally breeds only once a year, mating in late February or early March, but matings as late as June can occur.

The first person known to have bred wildcats in Britain was a Mr Alfred Heneage Cocks who lived near Hyde Park; he raised wildcat kits almost every year from 1875 to 1904. He was the first to set the gestation period at 65 to 68 days (since confirmed at 63 to 69 days) compared with the usual 58-63 days for the domestic cat, the females tending to give birth sooner if they had litters of four instead of two kits. He wrote to J.G. Millais, 'In captivity I have never observed a female Wild Cat come in season during the summer, but am not prepared to deny they may do so occasionally; but if so, I wonder it has always escaped my notice. Many years when, owing to the death of the young or the fact that the pair had not bred together in the spring, I have kept a male and female together all summer, they have shown no inclination to breed.'

In 1941 the zoologist L. Harrison Matthews wrote of examining several female wildcats, five of which were pregnant in late March and he rightly concluded oestrus must normally occur during the first half of March. But there was one lactating animal noted on May 25th which was also in oestrus, and another in lactation an-oestrus on August 29th. This early valuable evidence showed it was possible for wildcats to have more than one litter, though it does not prove that they do. Although Millais records perplexity at the sight of young Scottish wildcats in October which had clearly been born in late August or early September, the later scientific supposition that these kits 'must have been members of *second* litters born late in the summer' (my italics), is perhaps not correct. They could just as easily, and far more likely in my view, have been *first* litter kits born late. There could be many reasons; their mother might not have mated at all in the spring. I know that one of my females came into oestrus twice and another three times, up until late May at least, when they had not mated.

My own experience showed that wildcat kits are not fully weaned until three to three and a half months old: even the earlier-leaving female kits need to stay, run and learn survival techniques with their mother for at least three and a half months. Probably the kits stay with her for four or even five months, until they are big and strong enough, their claws sufficiently developed and hardened, to hunt on their own and scoot up trees from danger. It also takes them some time to learn efficient night hunting from their mother. The male kits seem to need their mothers longer — one of mine stayed close to his mother all through the winter and early spring too, when, during periods when both were free, he could easily have left. Millais also felt that kits born at the normal time (May) run with their mother until September. So the assertion that Scottish wildcats bear kits in May and a second litter about August seems unlikely and has not been proven.

Trying to shed some light on this controversy, I examined two papers on the zoo breeding of wildcats — from Berne Zoo, Switzerland, between 1960 and 1967; and from Prague Zoo, Czechoslovakia, from 1963 to 1967. It is interesting to note that out of the 32 litters (16 at each zoo) there were only *three* cases of two litters a year. (This substantiates Mathews' findings on late-lactation oestrus.) But the one Berne female who had kits in April and also in August 1961 died at the early age of four. The fecund female at Prague destroyed her first litter in the spring of 1963 but reared a second litter in August that year. In 1964 the same female cared for her spring litter until the kits were taken away from her in early June, then in August gave birth to a second litter of only one kit. But this kit died the day after its birth. Jiri Wolf, Prague's Curator of Mammals, comments: 'From this it can be deduced that, physiologically, she was unprepared to rear a second litter that year; but other factors may well have been involved'. It seems to me, too, that if things go wrong after the birth of second litters in zoos, how much worse would they be in the harsh conditions of the wild?

Berne Zoo director, Monika Meyer-Holzapfel, makes some pertinent comments. She records that they did not separate males from females when they had young 'for the female is sufficiently aggressive during this period to chase the male away from the nest box'. She also writes, 'The birth season lasts from March to August. This means if a birth occurs in August, it may not necessarily be the second litter of the year: it may equally be the first litter of the year.'

The young tom I gave to Edinburgh Zoo to mate with a lonely female they had there sired seven litters between 1978 and 1982, totalling 17 kits; not once were there two broods in one year. As Frances Pitt first pointed

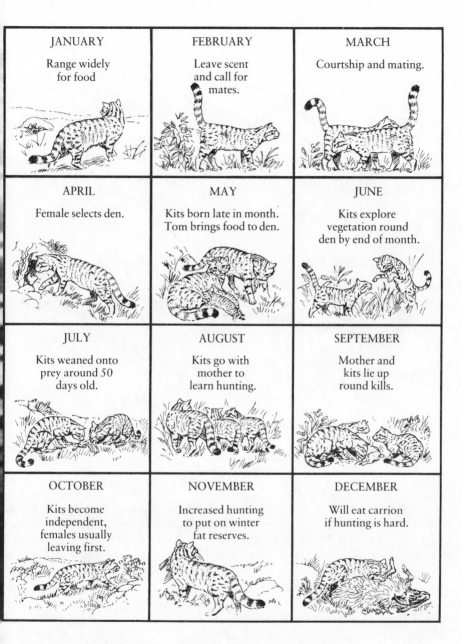

JANUARY	FEBRUARY	MARCH
Range widely for food	Leave scent and call for mates.	Courtship and mating.
APRIL	**MAY**	**JUNE**
Female selects den.	Kits born late in month. Tom brings food to den.	Kits explore vegetation round den by end of month.
JULY	**AUGUST**	**SEPTEMBER**
Kits weaned onto prey around 50 days old.	Kits go with mother to learn hunting.	Mother and kits lie up round kills.
OCTOBER	**NOVEMBER**	**DECEMBER**
Kits become independent, females usually leaving first.	Increased hunting to put on winter fat reserves.	Will eat carrion if hunting is hard.

The wildcat year.

Wildcat with kittens.

out — in the wild mountains of Scotland where life is strenuous, conditions are not as compatible with the rearing of offspring as in the free and easy life of well-fed domestic cats which can have even three litters a year. It is interesting that feral cats, which lead tougher lives than domestics (which have constant food and shelter in a house, garden or apartment) also tend to have just one litter a year. A study by Roger Tabor of feral cats in London (in which he also quotes the findings of the Dutch Feral Cat Foundation in Amsterdam, where densities of ferals were much higher than London) leads him to conclude: 'living wild the domestic cat is more like the wild cat in normally having only one litter per annum.'

Another point worth raising here is the behaviour of the wildcat female when rearing kits. My own female, despite good feeding, was considerably exhausted during the weaning of her kits and while I only once *saw* her drive off an approach by the tom during this period, it may have happened more often at night. It seems likely that if a mother in the wild came into late-lactation oestrus, with her kits about her, she too would drive off an interested tom.

Having late summer or autumn kits cannot be the norm for they would hardly be developed enough in time to cope with winter conditions. In May or June far more natural prey abounds — young birds, rabbits, hares, voles, mice, frogs and insects. Thus not only does the mother have less trouble hunting, feeding, rearing and teaching her kits but they also have more time to learn the techniques they need before the onset of winter. Spring kits receive a far better start in life.

From breeding and releasing my own animals and from the evidence of others, it does not seem possible for a wildcat to rear a family successfully in some two and a half months, then have another and rear that to survival. While possible, having a second, late litter seems extremely unlikely.

Development of young

Wildcat litters appear to vary considerably. At Berne the number of kit varied between one and eight, though still-birth was probable in large litters. The average litter size there was four. At Prague it was three. Of th two broods sired by my old tom, the average was three, and of the sever fathered by the young tom I gave to Edinburgh Zoo, the average wa 2.42. In the wild, consensus and my own experience indicates two to fou young as the norm. Generally, slightly fewer males are born than female (Cocks recorded 32 male to 37 female kits) both weighing about the sam — between 4 and 5 oz (120 and 150 g) — though there are uncommor exceptions. Males gain weight faster.

At birth the kits are fully furred, their mouths and tongues brigh crimson: their paw pads are pink but they darken to near black by thre months of age. The kits can crawl at two days and, at a week old, befor their eyes are open, instinctively try to spit and hiss at any strang disturbance. Between the tenth and thirteenth day the eyes start to oper varying with individuals, the whole process taking four days, with th mother helping by licking away the sticky secretions from the lids. Th bright china-blue irises last until about the seventh week, then a greeny grey tinge begins at the pupils, spreading outwards and banishing the blu in eight to ten days. This colour lightens to the final yellow-gold by abou five months old.

The kits gain weight at a rate less than 3½ oz (100 g) a week at first bu once the kits begin eating solid foods, the weight gain averages betweer 3½ and 9½ oz (100 and 270 g) a week. Sexual maturity is attained at ter months of age but breeding records indicate that females give birth mor usually at two years old — by which time all wildcats are fully grown.

Raising young

In addition to her aggression and bravery in defence of her young, the wildcat is a good mother. She keeps the den clean and does not take food inside the bed section. She rough-tongues the young kits' rear quarters, stimulating excretions which, when they are very young, she swallows. As with most carnivores, and predatory birds too, aggression and competitiveness are encouraged in the sense that the mother will make no particular effort to ensure a runty or weak kit gets its share of the teats. Yet she keeps an alert eye on them when they first start to walk, calling or carrying them back into the den with a firm jaw grip right round the whole neck if they stray too far. When her kits were about a month old, my first female left them in the den for long periods, which must happen in the wild when the mother has to hunt. During her absences the kits remained silent.

There is a popular belief that females prefer to rear young away from the tom who is liable to kill and even eat them. I found no evidence of this. My tom showed no belligerence whatever to the kits but my own fears made me keep them apart. This was easy to achieve; he was a good deal bigger than she was so I made a gate of such size between their pens that while she could get through to him, he could not get through into her enclosure nor den. The surprising thing was that several times he carried some of his own meat to near the gate for her and left it there, as if trying to help her feed the kits. Geoffrey Kinns once described a visit he made to Philip Wayre's wildlife park in Norfolk where there was a male and female wildcat in one enclosure, together with their two kits, all peacefully dozing in the sunshine. As he kept watch, taking pictures, Kinns saw the tom get up, carry a piece of meat over to the farthest kit and drop it in front of its nose. Then the tom patted the kit on the head with one paw, and started chewing another morsel of meat as if showing the youngster what to do! One Highland keeper told Kinns that he saw a male wildcat walking through the heather, leading a line of kittens with the female bringing up the rear, and he thought they were moving to a den. Unfortunately the man waited downwind of the den on another day, saw the male carrying in a rabbit, lifted his rifle and shot the animal. This was in the years when wildcats had no legal protection whatever. Frances Pitt also believed the sire wildcat helped hunt for the family, just like a dog fox.

I have been unable to find any authentic records of a tom killing kits in

Mother's tail tip trains kittens to pounce.

the wild or in zoos. If it does happen in the wild it is probably aberrant individual behaviour, or due to accidental meeting with a hungry tom, or later when kits are competing on the same territory. In the Berne and Prague zoo papers there is no record of a male attacking young, though there are several cases of mothers destroying and eating their own kits, particularly if the litter size was large. I cannot help feeling that the noise and disturbance that inevitably occurs in zoos could be a factor here, particularly with inexperienced females.

When the kits are weaning off onto meat from about six to seven weeks old, they follow the mother when she defecates and she appears to encourage them to cover droppings on soft surfaces, for they often copy her actions. She appears to slow down the raking actions of her paw, trying to make sure they can see what she is doing. When the kits are really mobile she helps them become strong and fast on their feet by much 'tail twitch' training. She lies down, sometimes for an hour or so at a time, and just airily flicks the black tip of her long tail about, while the kits tire themselves trying to chase and 'catch' it. This labour-saving method of kitten education can go on while she is sitting, standing or even eating. It is a clever device for it means the kits are extended yet the mother, tired and drained during weaning, expends no energy herself, or very little.

As the kits watch, she also 'catches' waving flowers, blowing leaves, crane flies and moths and fast-walking beetles, which seems the preliminary training for the kits to learn to hunt. Several times, with both litters, I saw the female catch voles, shrews and occasional birds that raided left-over food but instead of crippling them so they were half-alive, she killed them and only when dead did she drop them among the kits. Then she batted them about with her paws, deliberately encouraging the youngsters to chase after them. The first kit to catch this 'prey' then defended it with high whirring growls from the others, as if copying the growls its mother made when the weaned kits approached *her* too closely when she was eating.

The kits can walk, unsteadily, at about a month. After two more weeks they are surer on their feet and can climb a little at seven weeks. From two months they accompany their mother on short forays, then stay with her on longer expeditions, lying up then near covered kills in temporary dens. There seems little doubt that they often watch their mother hunting but how much they actually learn from this is guesswork. Hunting is instinctive in predatory animals, as even domestic cat owners know, and kittens taken from their mothers even before weaning is complete can become perfectly accomplished hunters without any parental guidance at all.

Enemies

A large fox might be cunning enough to snatch a kitten when it first started wandering away from its mother on brief independent outings from the age of ten weeks. Such predation, however, would be slight. (Foxes several times came near my wildcat litters when normally they never approached the cottage in summer.) Certainly, adult wildcats could easily repel a fox, or escape, their reactions being that much faster. The great Seton Gordon records several battles between eagles and wildcats in his book *Days With The Golden Eagle,* including one when the wildcat was so badly injured it ran round and round in circles in the snow before being shot by a stalker who followed its tracks. The eagle was also found dead later, with severe injuries on its neck. Wildcat kits have been recorded in eyries but very rarely, and in over 215 items of prey brought into west Highland eyries by golden eagles that I recorded over the years, not once did I find a wildcat kitten. They have been known to take smaller domestic cats gone wild, however, as Gordon also records, even feeding them to their chicks.

The fact is that the wildcat's main enemy has been (for as long as he has been around) *man,* and I am sure there are still a few boneheaded die-hards around who would shoot a wildcat if they had the opportunity. The animal continues to be sometimes persecuted on grouse moors and where low-ground game like pheasants and partridges are reared and preserved. Studies have shown, however, that just because predators kill grouse does not mean they affect total grouse numbers available for sport shooting. Wildcats can do more damage if they can get into the pens where large numbers of birds like pheasants are artificially reared and kept for release to the wild. But, as Dr Nigel Easterbee, of the Nature Conservancy Council, points out in *Lutra* (1988): 'This problem could be largely alleviated if greater care was taken over the siting and security of release pens, by following the advice given by the British Field Sports Society, Game Conservancy, Royal Society for the Protection of Birds, and the Wildfowlers' Association of Great Britain and Ireland. It could be argued that the onus should be on the game preserver to take all reasonable steps to prevent the ingress of predators to such an obviously highly concentrated and attractive source of food, rather than simply resorting to killing predators as a solution to the problem.'

Following a campaign to get the wildcat protected, an attempt to end the centuries of human persecution of the species was made in the 1981 Wildlife and Countryside Act. The wildcat was placed under Schedule 6, which stated that it could not be poisoned, trapped or snared, although it could still be shot. In any event, the Act was weakened by a clause that stated it would not be an offence to kill any wild animal or bird (except birds in Schedule 1) if it could be proved the action was necessary to prevent serious damage to crops, growing timber or fisheries. The situation for the wildcat was put right (at last) in 1988 as a result of the first 5-year review of the Act, when the wildcat, the porpoise, the dormouse and the pine marten were given full protection, and placed on Schedule 5. It is now an offence to injure, kill or take any of these animals from the wild.

Can a wildcat be tamed?

I would not recommend anyone to attempt to tame a wildcat — anyway, to take one from the wild is an offence. Even keeping one that has been reared in captivity requires a licence (because wildcats come under the Dangerous Wild Animals Act).

It is *just* possible to rear a wildcat to a degree of tameness, provided one gets it young, preferably before its eyes have opened, and one treats it with care and a deeply felt love. You cannot ever retaliate in kind no matter what the little spitball dishes out! I know of no one who has ever tamed a tom wildcat but females can be tamed enough for them to come indoors for food, allow themselves to be picked up (sometimes, not always) and occasionally to seek their owner's lap. They can not, however, be fully house trained. A wildcat marks or 'signs' parts of its territory with both faeces and urine and while it may go two weeks or so without using the room or rooms which are its shelter, sooner or later it will transgress. Its moods are more unpredictable than the more happy-go-lucky domestic cat; if it feels like being caressed or playing with some form of devised toy, it can resemble an outsize 'moggie' having fun, but if it does not it can reject any advance with a flaring hiss or even a spit. If it wants to be left alone it will growl a warning at the proffered hand.

I did manage to more than half tame a young female and she stayed with me up to the age of 2½ years, but she began to wander in oestrus in her second spring, and finally did not return. I was sure she wanted a tom. I had several advantages on my side when taming her, and I also played some downright cunning tricks. Firstly, she was a runt anyway and would have been kept off her mother's teats by the other three heftier kits in the competition for milk, had I not had all the time in the world to keep watch and manoeuvre her back onto them from time to time. In the wild she might have starved to death. She became used to my voice, my attempts to make wildcat mother sounds, before her eyes opened. I took her from the family as often as possible, keeping her in my bedroom overnight and feeding her well, only putting her back with the family so she could also keep getting some of her mother's milk, and receive the usual hunting and other training with the family. I cheated at times too. In the bedroom-study I gave her the finest foods and creamy milk to drink. When I put her back into the pens I filled the bowls with the coarsest meats and water and she did not think much of that. Later I would bring her indoors, give her

'Stuff the venison, what about some grouse for a change?'

the best of everything, then go out and feed the others the good foods too — which of course she knew nothing about. I must emphasize that I lived in an almost completely wild situation, with no roads, or neighbours, within six miles. Taming a wildcat, even partly, could not be achieved in an urban situation.

Can I see a wildcat?

In seventeen years of living in wild remote places in the Scottish Highlands, I only had ten sightings of wildcats actually in the wild, but I was more fortunate than most for I met many folk who had lived there all their lives yet had never so much as glimpsed one. Of those ten sightings, three came while driving a Land Rover along deserted single track roads, and one when I was working my way down between huge mossy boulders in a wood of tall conifers. Three more occurred when wildcats dashed across the road at night in my headlights, and three further sightings happened when I had gone deliberately to try and see one. Of these, the first occurred when I had seen a tom wildcat walking along one of his own trails at dusk; next dawn I stalked to the edge of a wood downwind and waited for him to hunt again. My hunch that he might use the same path again proved right. The second happened when I had waited downwind of a den, and the third when I and a keeper friend had set out offal bait and had waited at night some fifty yards away, also occasionally using a squeaker device imitating a distressed rabbit and the beam of a powerful torch in which to see the approaching cat. The latter method could have been repeated more times of course. It is a successful method once you have located signs of the wildcat but is better practised in winter, and one needs stamina for enduring the cold. On more than twenty occasions I have found signs of wildcats — footprints, scats, bird carcasses (remnants) with feathers torn and raked out, hay beds under rocks, and even three dens.

It is extremely unlikely for an amateur to see a wildcat in the wild during daylight; if you wish to try, look at the distribution map on page 95 and select an area where wildcats are shown to occur. Within this area, find the wildest terrain and search for signs such as those mentioned. It would be easier to see a wildcat in the autumn or early winter for at this time they are more likely to hunt by *day* as they need to put on extra fat to help them through the winter. When you find a likely looking open patch between heather, gorse bushes, trees or below big falls or slides of rocks, always approach upwind — so that the wind or breeze is blowing in your face and not from behind yourself to any animal before you. And if you can, time it for the sun to be behind you (if there is any sun) so that it dazzles the eyes of any animal looking in your direction. Move slowly, wear camouflage gear that matches the terrain, sit down between cover

and keep *quiet!* Also, be prepared for a wait of several hours. The wildcat is a rare, elusive and wary creature but in winter it is possible for it to take carrion laid down by man, provided you remove all human scent — boots and gloves should be dipped in boiled pine needle juice for example!

Dens are also difficult to locate, there usually being no sign of the animal's presence except a faint trail if grass is not too short. Occasionally, some feathers or a few skulls of birds and voles or other prey might be found nearby, but there is no smell, as there is with the fox. If you do find a den, do not go too close and certainly not on the day you intend to set up a watch. Get downwind, as far from the den as possible, while the terrain (bushes, rocks and so on), still affords a view; then just wait. One can be lucky in summer, for wildcats often emerge from their dens in the morning to bask on mossy rocks nearby, enjoying a warming of the old bones in the sunshine.

Do wildcats interbreed with feral domestics?

For over a century this question was the major controversy surrounding wildcats; the answer, perhaps sadly, is yes. In places like the less dense woodlands and the moors and lower mountain slopes, wildcats have mated with domestic cats roaming wild and have produced vigorous hybrids. I am convinced the pure breed still exists, in its wilder, remoter fastnesses. The point is, what impact has such interbreeding had upon total populations, and on the purity of the original race?

For many years a strong body of zoological and popular opinion held

Relative sizes of wildcat (outline) *and domestic cat* (foreground).

that wildcats and domestic cats, being different species, did not interbreed. It was known of course that big 'cats' so far apart as lions and tigers could mate, producing what were called ligers and tigons. As these offspring were infertile (could not have cubs), it was assumed any offspring of a liaison between wild and domestic cat would also be infertile. On the other hand, there was a smaller body of opinion that the wildcat population was heterogeneous, not homogeneous, the diverse elements being due to an admixture of domestic blood.

Way back in 1896 naturalist Edward Hamilton, after a 'careful examination of many pelts reputed to be wildcats' wrote, 'I found many indications of a mixture between the wild and domestic cat. It seems the original wildcat as it existed in olden days has been almost exterminated throughout Europe. Its place has been taken by a mongrel race, the result of continual interbreeding during many centuries . . .' He claimed the offspring *were* fertile, though he appeared to present no proof, but he went so far as to call the hybrids *Felis cattus feras*. His was a lone voice for many years. I earlier wrote that domestic cats must have come from a very large genetic pool. Given the obvious interbreeding between small wildcats in Africa and Asia, and bearing in mind man's shooting and trapping of thousands of Scottish wildcats over the years, is it not reasonable to believe that many, bereaved of their mates or unable to find a mate, would breed with receptive feral tabbies that they found on their territories, if they could?

Certainly it was shown around this time that wildcats *will* breed with domestics in captivity. Millais recorded Alfred Heneage Cocks as having bred some pretty hybrids from a male wildcat and a female domestic Persian cat in 1903, and again in April 1904 between a wildcat male and a female Abyssinian cat. Similar crosses, however, had been bred prior to 1873, by a Mr Pusey, of Pusey House, Berkshire, a 'handsome' pair of which he presented to the London Zoological Society. But, apparently, no one had yet found out if these crosses were fertile and could breed themselves.

The question remained unsolved until some light was shed in 1939 when naturalist Frances Pitt published *Wild Animals in Britain* (the first wildlife book I ever read). In it she recorded that she mated her male wildcat Satan to a domestic cat. She bred a number of hybrids which were not as fierce as their sire but 'inherited a considerable measure of his untamed spirit' and were 'nervous and queer tempered'. She added: 'These two cats will mate, and their offspring are fertile, but the hybrids show almost complete dominance of the wildcat type.' (By 'dominance' she was not referring to behaviour, but to inherited characteristics which were stronger in the hybrid.) She also stated that the offspring of the first cross (of the hybrids) showed 'throwbacks as regards coat pattern and length of fur to both the wild and domestic grandparents.' Looking back I am amazed that more was not made at the time by the zoological world of Frances Pitt's astonishing, and apparently pioneering, findings. At least, in his 1941 paper *Reproduction in the Scottish Wildcat* (1941) Harrison Matthews stated, 'Individual animals may show evidence of crossings by small size and thinly furred tails.'

Certainly, long before this, a few scientists had noticed that wildcats seemed to be getting smaller. In 1920 James Ritchie sought to establish that the animals had degenerated in size from Neolithic times. He cited measurements of ancient limb bones found at Dunagoil in Bute with those of more up to date animals:

	Prehistoric Wildcat	Modern Wildcat	Domestic Cat
Humerus (upper arm)	4¾ inches (120 mm)	4⅛ inches (106 mm)	3½ inches (90 mm)
Ulna (inner forearm bone)	5½ inches (140 mm)	4⅔ inches (119 mm)	4 inches (101 mm)
Femur (thigh bone)	5⅓ inches (135 mm)	4⅔ inches (119 mm)	4 inches (99 mm)

In an article in the *Scottish Field* in 1964, David Jenkins and David Stephen made a succinct suggestion: 'The true picture of in-between cats will never be clear until someone has bred wildcat to domestic, hybrid to hybrid, and wildcat to hybrid.' True enough, but I felt it would only be really clear if this crossing was to be done with a large number of cats over many years, so a reasonable facsimile of the genetic pool that exists in nature was achieved. It would be a costly and lengthy experiment, and far beyond my resources.

I tried to throw some modern light on the mystery, publishing the results in 1977. I examined the 88 pelts of wildcats classified as *Felis silvestris grampia* in the British Museum of Natural History in London, dating from 1867. I felt that if Scottish wildcats *had* been hybridizing significantly during the last hundred years some differences would show up. In the more recent or modern wildcats there should be a tendency towards the more tapering tails and fused, or blotched, tail-rings of the domestic cat, and also a gradual decline in the size of specimens. Omitting zoo and incomplete specimens, and what were obviously immature pelts, I recorded all the head and body and also the tail lengths, dividing the specimens into decades — from pre-1900 to the last dated skin in the collection — October 1946. The brief results below are interesting:

Average wildcat size from 1900 to 1950

Date	No. specimens	Head and body	Tail
pre 1900	7	25 inches (639 mm)	12¼ inches (310 mm)
1900-1910	10	22¼ inches (566 mm)	11 inches (279 mm)
1910-1920	9	22 inches (561 mm)	12¾ inches (324 mm)
1920-1930	10	22¾ inches (578 mm)	11⅜ inches (287 mm)
1930-1940	42	22½ inches (573 mm)	11½ inches (293 mm)
1940-1950	4	21½ inches (546 mm)	11¼ inches (285 mm)

'Recent wildcat', with tapered tail.

From these 82 specimens at least, it appeared that *overall* there had been a slight decline in size between 1867 and 1946. But I felt that for a fuller judgment, a far greater range of skins, including samples from 1946 to the present day, needed to be examined. I approached curator John B. Murray who sent me measurements of eleven pelts in the Royal Scottish Museum, Edinburgh, all taken between March 1957 and May 1959 in the Pitlochry region of Perthshire. The results showed a very small decrease in body size, and a slight increase in proportionate length of tail to body size in the pelts from the more recent years. There was also a far larger proportion of tapering tails and fused tail rings in the more recent pelts. I also noticed that six of the largest males in the British Museum collections had a fusing of the inner two of the four nape lines into a black patch. But this did not occur in any of the specimens after 1938, which were also smaller animals. In the mid 1970s I obtained three skins of wildcats that had been viciously trapped, run over and shot. The average head and body length was 22⅛ inches (562 mm); Tail: 11¹³/₁₆ inches (300 mm). Two of them had fused tail rings. Further and more 'personal' proof that wildcats will mate with domestics came with my own second female, which I had released down the loch in the summer. The following spring my Alsatian tracked her down by scent and put her up a tree. Realizing she was pregnant, I managed to live-trap her back and later she gave birth to four kittens with thin scrawny fused tails and piebald coloured coats. She had clearly mated with a big feral domestic black tomcat known to be in the area.

All the evidence so far made me side with Edward Hamilton and his belief that interbreeding had been occurring for centuries, for I found bused tails in wildcats as far back as 1886 and 1901, and tapering tails began as early as 1928.

The results of my investigation were printed in a book, *My Wilderness Wildcats*, in 1977. After it was published I was given a Christmas present of *The Handbook of British Mammals*, edited by G. B. Corbet and H. N. Southern, which came out later the same year. In the excellent section on wildcats by H. H. Kolb, I was surprised to learn that a Polish scientist, Pierre Suminski, had done similar research, also examining skulls, trying to measure what was pure or typical wildcat and what features had come from hybridization, and he had published the results in 1962 in Geneva in a paper: *Les caractères de la forme pure du chat sauvage, Felis silvestris.* After looking into pelage colouring and skull characteristics (35 skulls) he deduced that the average Scottish wildcat was 66 per cent pure, as compared to an average for Europe of 63 per cent. (The most pure were Polish wildcats at 73 per cent, while the least came from the Swiss and French Alps at 44 per cent).

Dr Kolb himself had also examined and measured Scottish wildcat skins (26 males and 16 females) dating from between 1958 and 1973 (which brought the statistics far more up to date) and he also recorded weights. He compared his results with those that Kirk and Wagstaffe published in 1943. Yet again, the decrease in body size (and weights) between the old wildcats and the more modern animals is obvious.

Measurements of Scottish wildcats

	Kirk & Wagstaffe 1919-1939	Dr Kolb's data 1958-1973	
	102 males	*26 males*	*16 females*
Head and body	589 mm (365-653)	564 mm (515-650)	543 mm (507-595)
Tail	315 mm (210-342)	307 mm (235-356)	293 mm (240-360)
Hind feet	138 mm (127-147)	134 mm (115-147)	126 mm (105-140)
Weight	5.1 kg (3.0-6.9)	4.7 kg (3.5-7.1)	3.9 kg (2.5-5.6)

While conducting this research, and breeding my own wildcats, I discussed the problem with my friend, the late Geoffrey Kinns, who,

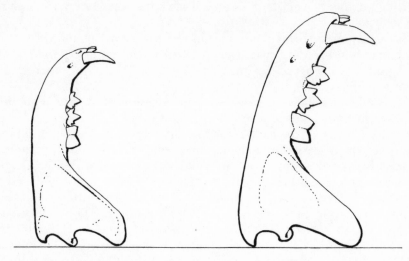

Jaw of domestic cat (left) *and wildcat* (right).

despite the loss of half a leg in World War II, was a brilliant wildlife photographer and possessed a large collection of British mammal and bird skulls. He said there was one sure way of telling whether a skull was that of a pure wildcat, a domestic or a hybrid. You take the bottom jaws (provided they are still fastened — or glued — together naturally) and stand them on a level surface on their broad rear ends, then let go. The wildcat jaws always stay upright, whereas the domestic or hybrid ones fall over! I have no idea how infallible this method is but it is based on the notion that the *ramus* bone in the domestic is always proportionately longer, causing the jaws to fall forwards – i.e. lower side downwards.

In 1982 the Nature Conservancy Council launched some serious investigation into the wildcat, including a survey of populations, run in the field by staff scientist Nigel Easterbee, who came to see me in May 1983. I gave him my ten sightings in the wild, the locations of tracks and signs and my two wildcat books which included results of my own researches. Before his tragic death in a car accident in December 1990 we remained in regular contact and he told me that they were proceeding steadily with the survey, difficult though this was with such a shy, cryptically coloured and nocturnal animal, and also looking into more foolproof methods of distinguishing wild, domestic and hybrid cats.

In 1987 the Institute of Terrestrial Ecology produced a complicated and horough paper by staffers Don French, Keith Corbett and Nigel Easterbee after their scientific study aimed at identifying populations of wildcats, domestics and their hybrids, by skull morphometrics. They examined the skulls of twenty-five 'old' (1901-1941) wildcats, fourteen 'recent' (1953-1963) wildcats, thirteen 'modern' (1975-1978) wildcats, twenty-four domestic (1976-1978) cats, and nine hybrids (1977-1978).

The differences in size that they discovered led them to make eight separate general conclusions:

'All analyses showed that "old" wildcats were different from all other groups.

'There was little or no difference between "recent" and "modern" wildcats. Both groups were separated not only from domestic cats, but also from "old" wildcats.

'The hybrid group was the most variable . . .

'Wildcats had larger, more robust skulls than domestic cats, and all the distinguishing variables were characters related to stalking, catching and killing of prey.

'Sexes were most distinct in "old" wildcats, less so in domestic cats and "recent/modern" wildcats, and least in hybrids, where the pattern of variation was also different from all other groups.

'We concluded that "old" wildcats were probably a (relatively) "pure" population of *F. silvestris*, but that "recent/modern" wildcat populations contained a (relatively) high proportion of hybrids.

'Most hybridization probably occurred earlier in this century, when wildcat numbers were low. [They point out earlier that feral cat numbers were relatively high around the 1940s]. The increase in "wildcat" numbers over the past 50 years or so may therefore include many hybrid cats. It was probably aided by increased afforestation in Scotland.'

At this point I was gratified that my theories of eleven years earlier had been proved largely correct but I was puzzled by their final conclusion:

' "Modern" wildcats tend to be slightly less like hybrids/domestic cats and slightly more like "old" wildcats than do "recent" wildcats, so the present trend may be to reduce hybridization; but it may be that the "pure" form of wildcat is effectively extinct in Scotland.'

This may sound like sitting on the fence, because if the first point is true, then the purer form must be coming back! However, it is difficult to see how any firmer conclusions could be reached, given the evidence. It is true that twenty of the twenty-five 'old' wildcats in the study came from Perthshire, which has provided most of the finest specimens in the collections, and none of the other cats in the other groups came from that area. However, there is no real proof that geographical location produces variation in skull morphology. The ideal study would be to obtain, say, ten animals in each of the seven groups from Perthshire, ten from Inverness-shire, and ten from Angus/Aberdeenshire area, a rather impossible task. Personally, after seventeen years of trekking the Scottish hills specifically searching for wildlife and nothing else, I believe the pure race of wildcat does still exist, but it is extremely rare.

Could the Exmoor 'beast' be a wildcat?

From the stories and conflicting accounts I have read in newspapers over the past twenty years, it could be anything from a feral dog, wolf, wolverine, leopard, puma, European lynx, or even an escaped staghound some hunt was keeping quiet about! It also seemed clear that it could be not just one 'beast' but several. The most frequent reported sightings were of large cat-like animals, though expert trackers and army patrols consistently failed to locate one.

The latest batch of sightings began in mid-April 1983 when Mike Hooper was woken at 2.30a.m. by the barking of his two boxer dogs at his home in Teignmouth, Devon. He switched on the lights and saw the orange-red eyes of a mysterious cat-like animal staring in at him. It loped round his secluded garden as he tried to see it by torchlight, then went through, or over, a 9ft hedge. Interest switched to Kingsbridge in south Devon in late May when three separate residents saw a

creature larger than a fox with a round cat-type face stalking through fields, one describing it as about 3ft high, of a golden brown colour and resembling a lion.

At the very end of May two schoolboys staying on an isolated farm in the heart of Exmoor saw what they described as a jet black animal, with white markings down its chest and bulging green eyes, prowling near a flock of sheep. Marcus White, 12, was quoted as saying, 'Its face was like an Alsatian with pale green eyes, but it did not move like a dog. It sort of pranced away.' By then about eighty sheep had been found killed by a big strong animal during the previous three months, and the Royal Marines sent out patrols containing marksmen to try to locate and ambush the animal. Many of the killings were in the South Molton area, and four days after a sheep was savaged at Ash Mill, a man saw a dark cat-like beast in the valley of the River Mole — shortly after he had been talking

to the soldiers! By the time he could report the sighting, of course, the 'beast' had vanished. From early June, sheep and lamb killings became less and less frequent, presumably because many forms of wildlife were burgeoning in summer and easy prey like new-born deer calves could be found farther away from the dangerous homes and herds of man.

At the end of June farmers at Manaton, near Bovey Tracey, Devon, were shocked when ten lambs were found killed, most with their heads torn off and bite marks were found showing canine teeth over two inches apart. While it could have been the work of a big dog on the loose, it was believed the concentration of the attacks purely on neck and head area showed the more skilled killing methods of a big cat. It could hardly have been the work of the 'beast of Exmoor' however, as Manaton is south-west of Exeter and is on the eastern edge of Dartmoor — from where, incidentally, other sightings of odd large cats had also been reported in recent years.

Naturally, in the spring of 1984 the farmers in the South Molton and Exmoor areas were worried for their flocks, after the previous year's losses of more than 100 sheep and lambs, even though the last known killing had occurred in October. To their relief there were no untoward slayings and some believed the 'beast' had not survived the winter.

But in October 1984 three men driving home to South Molton from work claimed they saw what looked like a black panther 'a lot bigger than an Alsatian, with a straight tail and a roundish face' near a quarry in the Bray Valley. They made a noise to scare it back into the open and it bounded out of a hedge, up a hill from the valley and vanished into bushy cover. One of the men said, 'It was like watching a big cat on a Survival programme.'

Later the same month, two well grown lambs were found killed on a farm near Buckfastleigh, once again on Dartmoor, this time on the south-eastern edge. The injuries were unlike those made by dogs. The front legs and shoulders were missing, the neck eaten down to the bone, and the sides were eaten down to the ribcage. The legend of the 'Beast of Dartmoor' was now also well founded. Speculation that it might be a wolverine, after 4-toed prints were found, ended rapidly when it was pointed out that a wolverine belongs to the same mustelid family as badger and otter — and has five toes, not four! A few more sightings and odd killings were reported over the next three years but nothing like the sheep deaths of 1983.

The first solid clue to the twenty-year-old mystery came in April 1988, after a lamb with its head ripped off was found on a farm near Widecombe on Dartmoor. The farmer kept vigil — and shot dead a large brown-spotted, yellow-gold coloured cat. The animal, almost twice the size of a big domestic cat, was identified at Paignton Zoo as a young adult leopard cat, normally found in south-east Asian forests where it preys on animals up to the size of young deer.

The animal could have been an escaped pet, or one 'released to the wild' by mistaken animal lovers. It could have been brought in illegally, without quarantine, when

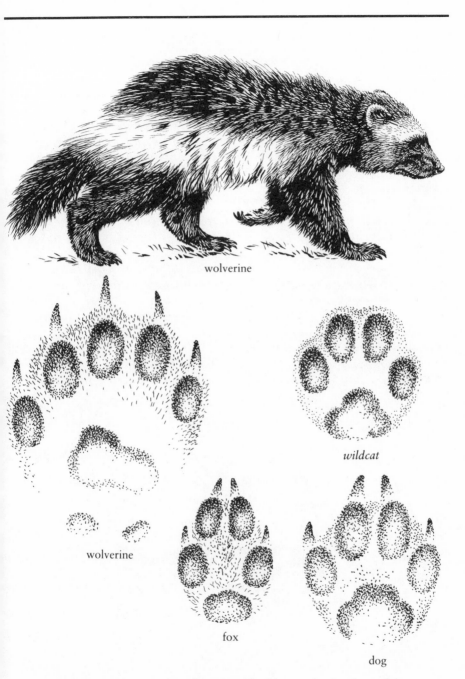

wolverine

wildcat

wolverine

fox

dog

Wolverine and comparative footprints of wildcat, wolverine, fox and dog.

little, and then abandoned on the moors when it became larger and the owner feared the police would find out.

It could well be that there is a nucleus of these, or similar, big cats breeding in the remotest parts of Exmoor and Dartmoor. Certainly, there is space and cover enough, with hills up to the height of 1,598 ft (487 metres) on Exmoor and the 2,038 ft (621 metres) High Willhays on Dartmoor.

In February 1989, farmer Norman Evans was walking through remote woodland near his country home outside Ludlow, Shropshire, when he found the body of a large sandy-coloured cat, some 3 ft long. It was later identified as a jungle cat, also known as the swamp cat, which inhabits Egypt and also south-east Asia. It was estimated to be about five years old but due to a severe injury on its back, possibly caused by collision with a road vehicle, it had probably been unable to hunt during its last days and had died of starvation. It only weighed 17 lb (8 kilos). While it was clearly not from Exmoor, it was further proof that large exotic cats can, and probably do, live in the wildest areas of Britain. When the laws on owning dangerous wild animals like big cats were tightened up a few years ago, there is little doubt that some misguided owners took their animals out to wild places and just let them go.

The answer to the question,

Leopard cat.

therefore, is that the 'Beast' of Exmoor, or of Dartmoor, or of anywhere else these kinds of sightings and killings occur, is certainly a 'wild cat'. But it is not the Scottish wildcat.

Remember the legendary story of the 'Surrey Puma' back in the 1960s, which first appeared in the Godalming area, spitting at a horrified council workman who was clearing thorny bramble bushes in a quiet area? Small livestock began to disappear, many sightings were reported (some of which were undoubtedly genuine) and police search squads called in Dr Victor Manton, Curator of Mammals at Whipsnade Zoo. Armed with a two-way radio and a tranquillizer rifle, he and the police hurried to places where the animal had been sighted. Once they thought they had the creature surrounded but the wood was just too impenetrable to search thoroughly. Dr Manton was surprised at just how many large dense woods there are in stockbroker-belt Surrey, often with plentiful stocks of rabbits and deer, and some of them quite big enough to hide a big cat for months or even years. Having, only two years ago, got temporarily lost myself in the seven miles of woodland round Leith Hill, I agree with him.

He believes the animal probably was a puma, otherwise known as cougar. They found a cluster of hairs on a barbed wire fence which exactly matched those on the tail of

Jungle cat.

a male puma; a local vet with much experience of African wild animals identified the wounds on injured goats as having been made by a large feline; and Dr Manton himself examined a newly killed roe deer where the body had suffered long and deep scratch marks and the neck had been broken instantaneously in a way not possible for a dog, fox or large feral cat. The Surrey puma was never found but maybe one day its skeleton or at least its skull, may be found by some intrepid trekker.

In 1988 evidence of another large 'cat' surviving in the wild came when a motorist knocked down and killed a large feline which was crossing a road at Hayling Island, Hampshire. On examination, it was found to be another 4 ft (1¼ metres) long African swamp cat.

There is believed to be another 'beast' in the Margam Forest of West Glamorgan, and in January 1990 a Daily Mail reporter confronted horse riders Ann Phillips, 43, and her 20-year-old daughter Lorna in the forest near their homes in Port Talbot. Mrs Phillips was sure she had seen a large puma and it was 'as big as a Great Dane' but it loped away from them down a track. Police and the National Farmers Union receive several calls a year about the Margam Beast worrying sheep.

How is the wildcat doing now?

Although there has been a considerable extension of range in Scotland since the turn of the century, the wildcat still only occupies a small part of its original range in Britain. This expansion is partly due to hybridization as well as a decrease in persecution (there was an 80 per cent decrease in the number of gamekeepers employed between 1871 and 1971). Re-afforestation has also helped the animal. There were estimated to be 33-37,000 hectares of forest areas in Scotland in 1914. With the establishment of the Forestry Commission five years later, plus the increased private tree planting, the area of forests had risen to 920,000 hectares (12.6 per cent of the land area) by 1982. The wildcat prefers a

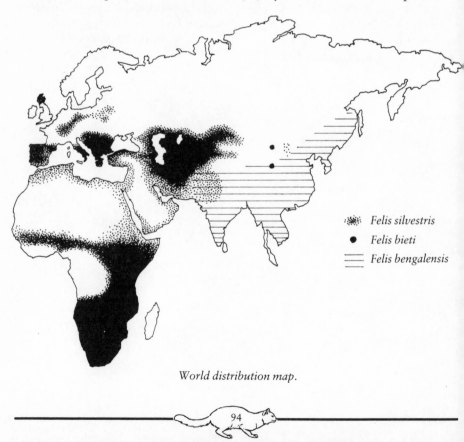

Felis silvestris
Felis bieti
Felis bengalensis

World distribution map.

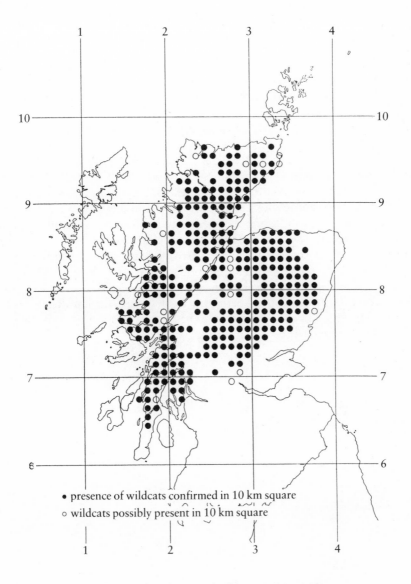

Scottish distribution of wildcats (NCC, 1988).

woodland habitat and, since it offers no threat to forestry interests (indeed it is 'useful' in its killing of voles), it is not persecuted at all in state-owned forests.

When the Nature Conservancy Council's modern survey of the wildcat (run by Dr Nigel Easterbee, to whom I am grateful for this information) began in 1982 it was thought that wildcats had re-conquered some of their old territories in south Scotland. However, the survey discovered that they had not. Today wildcats are found in most counties north of a line from Edinburgh to Glasgow but that relatively narrow central industrialized belt has proved too much of a barrier for the animals to cross. (See 1988 distribution map, page 95).

Once it had been proved beyond doubt that hybridization does occur, and has been happening more frequently in the last fifty or so years, some scientists believed the 'pure' form of wildcat was virtually extinct. However, a recent examination of a range of wildcat skulls by Nigel Easterbee indicates that while hybrids are present, animals similar to the old pure form do still exist (see page 85). I am sure the pure strain has survived, particularly on the highest ground, in the densest woodlands, and the remoter areas of the north and west where human density is low and domestic cats have not penetrated. In Britain as a whole, however, the wildcat is still an extemely rare animal.

Mystery black cats

While the mystery of the various 'beasts' can be explained by the release, or escape, of such large felines, what can we make of the large number of reported sightings that can *not* be so explained? We come now to the riddle of the Big Black Cats.

In the early 1980s reports of sightings of large black cats started coming in from the remoter regions of Britain, including, incredibly, one from near Frant, Kent. A farmer claimed he saw the animal, about the size of a labrador, cross a muddy farm track in front of his car. He said it had large yellow eyes and a long black tail. Most of the reports, however, came from the Scottish Highlands, particularly from the Grantown, Forres-Elgin, and Moray areas, and it was said the creatures had a predilection for chickens, ducks, and lamb chops that didn't fight back! They all had these large bright yellow, or golden, eyes and long thick tails, and were black all over. Popular theories held that they were young black panthers that had bred

Stalking lamb chops that don't fight back.

and been released by wildlife-loving zealots, or that they were even a 'new' species, hitherto undiscovered by man.

Several of my readers wrote to ask my opinion as to what they were, and to each I replied that I did not think they were panthers, nor that they were a newly discovered species. I was sure they would prove to be hybrids — crosses between wildcats and feral domestics. The black colour would come from a feral female and the large size, and golden eyes, from a wildcat male. Several of these big black cats were shot, and one of them was known as the 'Kellas cat'. It was shot by Tomas Christie of Kellas in 1983 close to the river Lossie, near Dallas, Morayshire. It was stuffed and mounted in a ferocious pose and is now on exhibition in Elgin Museum. After being mounted it was submitted for identification by naturalist/ author Di Francis and Mr T. Newton to the Natural History Museum, London. (I am grateful to Dr Daphne M. Hills, of the Museum, for these notes on the 'Kellas cat' and also of the 'Advie cat' which follow.)

The fact that the 'Kellas cat' had been mounted caused a few examination difficulties but it was found the head and body length, taken 'over the curves' was 25½ inches (650 mm), and the tail length was 11¾ inches (300 mm). The greatest skull length was 4 inches (105 mm). The tibia measured 5½ inches (144 mm) and the ulna about 5½ inches (140 mm).

While all these measurements are within the known range of the pure wildcat, this was a very big cat indeed. They are at the upper end of the range recorded for British wildcats, and approach in size those of the 'Ardgay cat', which is the biggest specimen in the museum's collection (weighing 15 lb 10 oz). Dr Hills's notes proceed:

'In summary the dimensions of this specimen are suggestive of a large British Wild Cat. We have no record of a black wild cat from this country although they have been recorded elsewhere.

'Black colour morphs of wild species of mammals are not uncommon. Other colour morphs also exist e.g. albinos. These odd specimens are not regarded as being different species and even when the morph appears relatively frequently in an individual population they have no taxonomic significance. Many examples exist in the British mammal fauna. White moles, shrews and hedgehogs are occasionally reported, as are black rabbits, squirrels, some voles and mice. Black cats of various species have been reported from many parts of the world.

'The best known black wild cats are those named *Felis daemon* by Satunin (1904), based on skins and skulls from the Caucasus and now in the Zoological Museum of the Academy of Sciences, St Petersburg. The

Big black cat.

specimens were subsequently examined by Smirnov (1917) who considered them to be melanic Caucasian wildcats (*Felis silvestris*) and by Ognev (1935) who identified them as feral domestic cats but acknowledged the possibility of the existence of melanistic forms of the Caucasian wildcat population. The measurements given by Satunin fall within the range of domestic cats and are smaller than those of the Kellas cat. Alekperov (1966) reported that out of a collection of 117 wildcat skins examined in a warehouse at Baku (Caucasus) in 1948, 14 were totally black and 3 were dark brown. *Felis daemon* is currently regarded as a synonym of *Felis catus* (domestic cat) following Ognev (1935).

'Discrimination between wild and domestic cat is not always simple and is even more difficult when only part of the specimen is available . . . Thus although the available evidence suggests that the Kellas cat is a black morph of *Felis silvestris* the possibility that it might be a very large feral domestic cat or a hybrid between wild and domestic cats cannot be ruled out.'

In April 1985 another large black cat was shot by Mr L. Mallinson, gamekeeper, near Advie, which is eight miles from Grantown on Spey. This specimen was presented to the museum as it was, also by Mrs Di Francis, and the mammal section were asked for a report. This was made by Dr Daphne Hills (in consultation with Dr Nigel Easterbee and Dr Don French).

The 'Advie cat' was found to be a male, slender but well muscled. Its coat was less dense and had longer guard hairs than the 'normal' wildcat. The single long white body hairs it had are found in both wild and domestic cats. Similarly its white inguinal spots, but its tail was less bushy than the normal wildcat tail. In a very detailed report, Dr Hills also wrote:

'The gut length of the Advie cat was 135 cm. Haltenorth (1957) established that the gut length of the domestic cat exceeds 200cm. The gut in the wild cats is usually less than 150cm. Easterbee (pers. comm.) states that the gut length of hybrid animals is also usually less than 150cm.' The Advie cat weighed 4.35 kg which is rather below average for an adult wildcat. She concludes:

'The size, skull length, cranial capacity and gut length of the Advie cat are well within the range for the Scottish wild cat and the multivariate analysis supports this diagnosis. However, some skull characters and the coat length suggest an affinity with the domestic cat. It would thus appear that the specimen is not a melanic pure-bred wildcat but an individual with some domestic cat in its ancestry.'

Slowly, the truth about the Big Black Cats was being tracked down. But there was still no *real* proof of my theory, as expressed to readers, that they would prove to be crosses between wildcats and feral domestics. In a personal note, Dr Hills emphasized that it had not been possible to provide chromosome analyses in either case. The genetic origin of the big black cats was still ultimately a mystery.

In August 1986 a reader, Betty Gibson of Barton-on-Sea, Hampshire, wrote to me that she had seen a *Tomorrow's World at Large* programme on BBC television in which producer Martin Hughes-Games, working with keepers, had caught one of the big black cats and had made the whole programme about them. She wrote 'They had permission to try and catch one of the big cats to film, on condition they didn't release it in the same place. The cat was caught, anaesthetised, blood tested, and, as *you* said, found to be a hybrid of wildcat and domestic.'

Having had no electricity in my remote homes for 23 years, I did not see a video of the programme for almost a year, but it was fascinating. The genetic department of Aberdeen University had taken blood samples from a wildcat, a domestic cat and one of the big black cats, and had evolved a method of isolating and photographing the make-up of their respective chromosomes. The programme indicated that the black cat was a cross between a wildcat and a feral domestic (though this impression somewhat overemphasized the results the university was obtaining). Apart from solving the great mystery, this also gave even further convincing proof that the two species interbreed.

The big beautiful black cat was *not* released in the same place either. Martin Hughes-Games gave it to the Highland Wildlife Park at Kincraig near Aviemore, to keep company in a large treed enclosure with two normal wildcats — and I saw her there when I went to film an episode for the TV series *Animals Roadshow*.

Selected bibliography

Cocks, Alfred Heneage, 'Wildcats; Period of Gestation', *Zoologist*, 2nd Series, vol. XI (1876)

Cocks, Alfred Heneage, 'Wildcat Breeding in Confinement', *Zoologist*, 3rd series, vol. V (1881)

Corbett, L. K., 'Current research on wildcats; why have they increased?' *Scott. Wildlife*, 14: 17–21 (1978)

Corbett, L. K., *Feeding ecology and social organization of wildcats* (Felis silvestris) *and domestic cats* (Felis catus) *in Scotland*. PhD thesis (Aberdeen University, 1979)

Easterbee, Nigel, 'The Wildcat (Felis Silvestris) In Scotland: 1983 – 1987', *Lutra*, vol. 31 (1988)

Easterbee, Nigel, L. V. Hepburn and D. J. Jefferies. 'The Wildcat (Felis Silvestris) In Scotland: 1983–1987', *Survey of the distribution of the wildcat in Scotland 1983–1987* (Nature Conservancy Council, Peterborough, 1989)

French, D. D., L. K. Corbett and N. Easterbee., 'Morphological discriminants of Scottish wildcats (Felis silvestris), domestic cats (F. catus) and their hybrids. '*Journal of Zoology*, 214: 235–259 (1988)

Gordon, Seton, *The Golden Eagle* (Collins, London, 1955)

Hamilton, Edward, *The Wildcat of Europe* (R. H. Porter, London, 1896)

Hewson, R., 'The Food of Wildcats (Felis sylvestris) and Red Foxes (Vulpes vulpes) in West and North-East Scotland', *Journal of Zoology*, 200 (2); 283–289 (1983)

Hills, Daphne M., 'Black Cat from Advie, Scotland', British Museum (Nat. Hist.) Museum, unpublished report (1986). Also 'The Kellas Cat', by same author.

Jenkins, David, 'The Present Status of the Wild Cat (Felis sylvestris) in Scotland', *Scott. Naturalist*, vol. 70 (1961)

Kirk, J. C., and R. Wagstaffe, 'A Contribution to the study of the Scottish Wildcat (Felis silvestris grampia, Miller)', *N. West Nat.* 18: 271 – 275 (1943)

Kurten, Bjorn, *The Evolution of the European Wildcat* (Helsinki University, 1965)

Matthews, L. Harrison, *British Mammals,* Collins, London (1968) Also: 'Reproduction in the Scottish Wildcat', *Proceedings of the Zoological Society,* series B, vol. 3 (1941)

Meyer-Holzapfel, Monika, 'Breeding the European Wild Cat at Berne Zoo', *International Zoo Yearbook,* no. 8 (1968)

Millais, J. G., *The Mammals of Great Britain and Ireland* (Longmans Green, London, 1904)

Pitt, Frances, *Wild Animals In Britain* (Batsford, London, 1939)

Ritchie, James, *The Influence of Man on Animal Life in Scotland* (Cambridge University Press, Cambridge, 1920)

St John, Charles, *The Wild Sports of the Highlands* (1846; reprinted John Murray, London, 1907)

Stephen, D. and D. Jenkins, 'Wildcat', *Scottish Field* (March, 1964)

Suminski, P., 'Les caractères de la forme pure du chat sauvage Felis silvestris, Schreber', *Archs Sci.,* 15:278–296 (1962)

Volf, Jiri, 'Breeding the European Wild Cat at Prague Zoo', *International Zoo Yearbook,* no. 8 (1968)

Index

Figures in bold type refer to illustrations

Aberdeen 25, 28, 86
Abyssinian hybrid 80
Advie 100
Angus 25, 28, 86
annual cycles 65
Ardgay cat 98
Ardnamurchan 32
Argyll 25, 28, 29
Ash Mill 86
author's own wildcats, 9-10, 11, 22, 31, 36, 46-7, 48, 55, 58, 62, 64, 67, 68, 74, 82
Ayrshire 28

badger 34, 58
baldness cure 24
Banff 25, 27, 28, 29
barn owl 38
basking 50, **51**, 77
beetles 38, 71
Berwick 27, 29
big black cat 97, **99**
birds 38, **39**, 71
birds' nests, dens in, 49, 56
birth 58, 63
bite 87
black-throated divers **46/7**, 48
Bleadon caves 23, **26**
bobcat 30
Brown, Harvie 25

Caithness 28
carrion 31, 40, **65**, 77
cattus 12
Caucasian wildcat 99
chaffinch 37
chin 20
claws 17, 34, 44, 47, 48, 55, 56, **57**, 64

climbing 49
Cocks, Alfred Heneage 63, 80
Corbett, Keith 85
Creswell Crags, Derbys, 24, **26**

Dartmoor 88, 90
defence of kittens 34, 69
dens **52**, 56-7, **65**, 69, 71, 76, 77
distribution:
   historically in England 23-5
   historically in Scotland 25-9
   currently in Scotland 94-6
   throughout the world 30, **94**
dog 11, 33, 86, 88, **89**
domestic cat 11, 15
   differences between domestic and wildcat 17-21, 34, 60, 71, 74, 78, 84
   differences in hunting 42, 44, 46
   differences in burial of scats 52
   differences in breeding 63, 66, 83-7
   interbreeding with wildcats *see* hybrids
droppings *see* faeces
duck 38, 60
Dumbarton 27
Dumfries 27, 29

eagle 28, 34, **35**, 60, 72
ears 20
Easterbee, Nigel, 72, 84, 96, 100
Edinburgh 96
eels 38
eggs 48, 49
Egyptian cat figure **11**
Egyptians 11
Elgin 27
England 25
European wildcat 30
Exmoor 'beast' 86-91

extinction in England 25
eyes 20, 59, 68, 98

faeces **24**, 40, **52**, 54, 69, 71, 76
  burial of 52, 71
Felis cafra 12
Felis lunensis 15
Felis lybica 12, 13
Felis margarita 12
Felis ornata, 12, 13
Felis silvestris grampia 81
femur 81
feral cats 56, 66, 80, 83, 98
fights 36
fish **38**, 47
flank shape 17
food 37-40
  beetles 38, 71
  birds 38, **39**, 71
  carrion 31, 40, **65**, 77
  eels 38
  eggs 48, **49**
  fish **38**, 47
  frogs 38, **39**
  game 37, 72
  grasshoppers 38, 47
  hares 37, **39**, 46
  insects 38, **39**
  lambs 25, 38, 41, 88
  lizards 25, 31, 38
  mice 12, 37, 44, 46
  moles 38
  moths 38, 48, 71
  poultry 41, 42
  rabbits 28, 32, 37, 38, **39**, 42, **43**, 44,
    56, 91
  rats 13, 38
  red-deer calves 42
  roe-deer kids 42
  shrews 31, 37, **39**, 71
  slow worms 31, 38
  squirrels 38
  vegetation 40

voles 28, 37, **39**, 44, 46, 71
water voles 38, 47
weasels 38
forelegs 17
Forestry Commission 28, 94
fox 31, 32, 34, 49, 52, 56, 60, 72, 77, 81
Francis, Mrs Di, 98, 100
French, Don, 85, 100
frogs, 38, **39**
fur 17, 33, 34, 80

game birds 37, 72
gestation 63
Glasgow 96
Godalming 91
Gordon, Seton, 72
grasshoppers 38, 47
Grays Thurrock, Essex, 23, **26**
grouse 72, **75**
growling 33, 34, 46, 60, 61, 71
growth of kits 68
guard hairs 17
gut 100

habitat 57-8, 76, 96
Hamilton, Edward, 17, 24, 79, 83
hares 37, **39**, 46
Harmer, S.F., 25
Hayling Island 93
hearing 31, 46
Highland Clearances 25
Hills, Dr Daphne M., 95, 100
humerus 81
hunting 32, **41**, 43-50, 56, 64
hybrids 78-86, 96, 98-9, 101
  Abyssinian 80
  Persian 80

Ightham, Kent, 23, **26**
inguinal spots 100
insects 38, 48
Institute of Terrestrial Ecology 84
Inverness 25, 27, 28, 29, 86

jaws 34, 46, 84
Jenkins, Dr David, 28, 81
jungle cat 90, **91**, 93

Kellas cat 98-9
Kincardine 27, 29
Kingsbridge 86
Kinns, Geoffrey, 34, 69, 83
Kintyre 28, 29
Kirkcudbright 27
kits 58, 59, 60, 63, 64, **65**, 66, 67, 68, 69,
   82
   calls 50-60
   size of litter 68
   development 68
   training for hunting 70-71
Kolb, H. H., 83

lactation 63
lambs, killing of, 25, 38, 41, 88
Lanark 29
leopard cat 86, 88, **90**
lip smacking 59
lips 20
lizard 31, 38
Ludlow 90
lynx 30, 60, 86

'M' mark 20
MacNally, Lea, 32
Mallinson, L., 99
Mammal Society 29
Manaton 87, 88
Manton, Dr Victor, 91, 93
Margam Forest 93
marking territory 52, 54-5, **56**
mating 10, 54, 61, 63
Matthews, L. Harrison, 63, 64, 80
measurements 21, 22, 81-3
merganser 38
mice, 12, 37, 44, 46
Millais J. G., 46, 49, 63, 64, 80
moles 38

Moray 27, 29
moths 38, 48, 71
moult 20
Murray, John B., 82

Nairn 27, 29
Nature Conservancy Council 29, 72, 84, 96
Neolithic 80
nose 17, 20

oestrus 54, 60, 61, 63, 64, 67, 74
otter 34

pairing 62
Palladius 14
panther 12, 97, 98
Pasht 11
paws 9, 40, 68
persecution 24, 25, 57, 72-3
Persian/wildcat hybrid 80
Perth 29
Perthshire 29, 85, 86
Phoenicians 11
Pitt, Frances, 62, 64, 69, 80
play 47, 61, 71
predation 72
prey *see* food
poultry 41, 42
puma 12, 20, 54, 60, 86, 91, 93
pupil 20, 68
purr 60
Pusey 80

rabbits 28, 32, 37, **39**, 42, **43**, **44**, 56, 91
rabbit squeaker 32, 76
rats 12, 38
Ravenscliff, Glam., 24, 26
rearing young 69
   role of tom 69-71
   tail-twitch training **70**, 71
   teaching hunting 47, **65**, 71
reproduction 54, 63-7
Ritchie, James, 25, 80

Romans 12, 14
Ross & Cromarty 27, 28, 29

scent 31, 32, 47, 77
Scottish wildcat 15, 16, 30, 64, 80, 83, 91, 100
screech 60
sheep killing 87, 88
shrews 31, 37, 39, 71
sight 31, 44
skins 23, 24, 81, 82, 83
skull 18/19, 34, 83, 84, 85, 96
slow worm 31, 38
South Moulton 86, 88
spitting 9, 33, 59, 60
spraying see marking territory
squirrels 38
St John, Charles, 34
Step, Edward, 25
Stephen, David, 81
Stirling 27, 28, 29
summer coat 20
Sunderland 29
Surrey puma 91
Sutherland 27, 29
swamp cat see jungle cat
swimming 48

Tabor, Roger 66
tail 20, 33, 34, 81, 91
    tapered 81, 83
    tail ring 81, 83

teeth 17, 34, 40, 44, 87
terns 48
toe pads, 17, 88
tongue 20, 68
tracking 76
tracks 21, 48, 57, 76, 89

ulna 33, 81
urine 52, 54

value of cats 14-15
vegetation 40
voice 59
voles 28, 37, 44, 46, 71

watching wildcats 76-7
water voles 38, 47
weaning 63, 67, 71
weasel 38
whiskers 20, 32
Widecombe 88
Wigtownshire 27
Wildlife and Countryside Act 73
wolf 86
wolverine 86, 88, 89
woodpigeon 37
wood wasp 40

zoos 64, 68, 71
    breeding of wildcats in 64
    Edinburgh Zoo, 64, 68
    London Zoo 9

If you have enjoyed this book, you might be interested to know about other titles in our **British Natural History** series:

BADGERS
by Michael Clark
with illustrations by the author

BATS
by Phil Richardson
with illustrations by Guy Troughton

DEER
by Norma Chapman
with illustrations by Diana E. Brown

EAGLES
by John A. Love
with illustrations by the author

FROGS AND TOADS
by Trevor Beebee
with illustrations by Guy Troughton

GARDEN CREEPY-CRAWLIES
by Michael Chinery
with illustrations by Guy Troughton

HEDGEHOGS
by Pat Morris
with illustrations by Guy Troughton

OWLS
by Chris Mead
with illustrations by Guy Troughton

RABBITS AND HARES
by Anne McBride
with illustrations by Guy Troughton

ROBINS
by Chris Mead
with illustrations by Kevin Baker

SEALS
by Sheila Anderson
with illustrations by Guy Troughton

SNAKES AND LIZARDS
by Tom Langton
with illustrations by Denys Ovenden

SQUIRRELS
by Jessica Holm
with illustrations by Guy Troughton

STOATS AND WEASELS
by Paddy Sleeman
with illustrations by Guy Troughton

URBAN FOXES
by Stephen Harris
with illustrations by Guy Troughton

WHALES
by Peter Evans
with illustrations by Euan Dunn

Each title is priced at £6.95 at time of going to press. If you wish to order a copy or copies, please send a cheque, adding £1 for post and packing, to Whittet Books Ltd, 18 Anley Road, London W14 OBY. For a free catalogue, send s.a.e. to this address.